The Witch-ionary

··❯❯ ◗ ○ ◖ ❮❮··

An A-Z of magickal terms and their meanings

Deb Robinson

DAVID & CHARLES
—PUBLISHING—

www.davidandcharles.com

Contents

Merry Meet
4

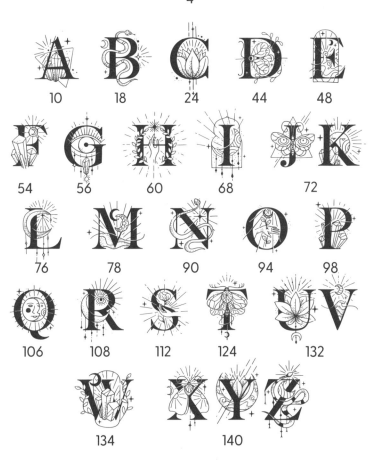

A 10   B 18   C 24   D 44   E 48

F 54   G 56   H 60   I 68   JK 72

L 76   M 78   N 90   O 94   P 98

Q 106   R 108   S 112   T 124   UV 132

W 134   XYZ 140

About the Author
142

RITUALS

16 Casting a Magick Circle

23 Self-Love Charm Bag

43 Distance Healing Spell Powder

59 Heart-Healing Bath Soak

67 Setting Boundaries Candle Spell

70 Simple House Blessing or Cleansing

74 Know Your Worth Confidence Spell

89 Anti-Anxiety Salts

93 Negativity Banishing Potion

97 Wish Come True Candle Spell

111 Past Relationships Cleansing Spell

123 Letting Go Fire Ritual

131 Calming Bath Ritual

Merry Meet

Many people ask me how old I was when I discovered I was a witch, but for me there was no defining moment; I have always, since I was a child, believed in magick. I suppose the difference between me and most other children is that I never stopped believing in it! I was born in Yorkshire, England, into a working-class family, and brought up to appreciate every gift life has to offer. My three siblings and I were raised to see the potential in all things. While my father was out working hard to make a living, my mother would craft for hours making hand-made clothes for our Sindy dolls, and wooden furniture far superior to the plastic offerings the department stores had for sale. She would often take everyday items and turn them into enchanting toys. We didn't for a minute think that this was born of necessity, we simply felt blessed with what we had, with nothing, somehow; because of the love our parents had for us, we had everything!

Every task in our house was turned into a game, so that I and my elder sister Angela, elder brother Jay-Jay, and twin sister Sam, had a childhood so filled with joy it was hard to imagine wanting for anything!

Though my parents were not witches, we were nevertheless raised on fairy stories, fantasy and magick. Nothing was ordinary: sticks were magick wands, rugs were flying carpets (which only worked when you shut your eyes, of course!), dandelion clocks were for wishes, daisies for divination; the everyday world had endless magick, and we were taught to look for it and to believe in it.

Having a twin sister, I'm convinced, is what made me such an empath. What she felt I felt, be it physical pain or emotional. We have always felt each other's woes and joys as if they were our own – because in fact, they were. Through this I have learnt to really, truly notice and care about how others feel, and not just people but animals too.

I married my childhood sweetheart, Lenny, at seventeen, and we have three children, Steven, Ella and Ralph. The most important gift we gave to them was self-belief, and we taught them the power of it – that this self-belief has magickal powers strong enough to manifest your heart's desires! And because of this self-belief, each of them is fulfilling their dreams.

Although I had always studied witchcraft and divination, after hearing the rumours that my maternal great, great grandmother was a 'fortune teller', who would travel from place to place reading tarot, I was inspired to take up tarot reading myself. I was awed when I discovered my own natural ability to read intuitively, and from that moment I really started to focus on my own witchcraft journey and to truly identify as a witch.

After some time, having become so passionate about the craft, we opened our beautiful family-owned magick emporium, Practical Magick, in the heart of Yorkshire, England. It was a bustling little shop filled with love, warmth and positive energy, a place embraced so warmly by those from all spiritual paths that people would even come from overseas to pay us a visit, and to have me read their tarot cards – such was Practical Magick's reputation!

In November 2016 my daughter, Ella, and I launched our magickal monthly subscription box, Witch Casket, and we could not have known then that it would become so popular so quickly! It was with light and happy hearts we closed the doors of Practical Magick in February 2017 to focus on Witch Casket full time; knowing that we had not suffered one day of stress and anguish there, that it had been perfect from beginning to end. We were so happy to be closing because of success, rather than failure – and overjoyed to realise that there are so many magickal people worldwide.

To this day, with Witch Casket, we continue to sprinkle our magick, not only here in Yorkshire, but all across this glorious planet. It is heart-warming to know that witches worldwide are learning from my lifetime of study and knowledge, performing my tried and trusted spells and rituals, working with the divination tools that I have created, and being empowered to live their authentic, magickal lives.

And more than ever, today, witchcraft runs through everything I do. I believe that if we can control our thinking, and radiate the energy of someone living a more joyous life, we can attract that joyous life to us. Our thoughts are like placing our order to the universe, so we should place our orders wisely! It's impossible to be positive 24/7 of course, but having faith that when things go wrong, we are learning and growing, and that things will improve; that in itself helps to bring positive change.

I think it's essential to know that the most important things in witchcraft are our own intent and belief, that's our magick! If we

MERRY MEET

intend something, and we truly believe in it, and we work hard towards it, it will be ours. But if we don't set that intention, or have that belief, no amount of hard work can bring us our desired outcome. Once you know your power, nothing can stop you!

I think there is an enormous need to feel more empowered. So much feels out of our control right now, and there is so much negativity around, so it's understandable that so many people want to explore witchcraft and find their power. Additionally, with so much focus on the media, image, material possessions etc, turning back to a more natural way of living feels like a beautiful act of rebellion! Taking a step back from the chaos to meditate, to take a ritual bath, or work with herbs, essential oils, and crystals, to research, to write, and to heal... doesn't that sound irresistible?

As I've followed my path, it's become clear that witchcraft has a unique and fascinating lexicon. For those new to witchcraft, it can be a path paved with confusion. Some of the terminology used may leave you unsure or even overwhelmed. Those starting their magickal journey will often devour dozens of books in their quest for knowledge, but in reading those books can find themselves frustrated by the continual use of words they may not have come across before, and this hinders their learning. As an experienced, practicing witch who offers spells, rituals and guidance to witches worldwide, I have lost count of the times I've been asked to write this very book!

With these requests in mind, I have created *The Witch-ionary;* a collection of over 200 of the most common magickal terms

and their definitions. And where I found it could be useful, I've also included some instructions or examples. Some of the words in this book may not relate directly to witchcraft but are used often enough in witchcraft circles that I deemed it important to include them. After reading this book, and learning the meanings of the most frequently-used words and phrases, you will find yourself more able to study the craft without impediment. While writing this book, I romanticised about witches worldwide curling up in front of a roaring fire with a witches' brew, their familiar by their side, and consuming book after magickal book without stumbling over previously undiscovered words and obscure phrases. It was this thought that motivated me to compile this useful, informative guide.

While reading *The Witch-ionary*, you will develop your understanding of the magickal words included, why we use them, when we use them, what they truly mean (as in some cases they may be used out of context by those not within the magickal community), and the weight that they carry. Many of these words are rooted in magickal history spanning centuries, carry deep cultural significance and should be respected as such. If a word is in any way controversial, or it relates to a closed practice, I have been mindful to include this information. And it should be noted that though I offer a definition, I do not offer my personal opinion; nor do I offer or promote my own religious or spiritual beliefs – everyone's path is unique and valid. The beauty and magick of witchcraft is that it follows no set path, and has no hard and fast rules, rather, it is a labyrinth through which we each find our own path, learning and growing as we go. I hope you find this book to be a useful guide on your own witchcraft journey.

Aeromancy

A form of divination in which the air and atmospheric conditions are interpreted. Insight is gained from observing the shape of the clouds, the weather, the wind, etc. Since ancient times people have observed the weather, believing it to be a medium through which the gods communicate their feelings. Some fortune tellers still look to the skies for messages from the Divine. Aeromancy is a very intuitive form of divination, so look up to the sky, tap into your subconscious mind, and let your intuition guide you.

Affirmation

The assertion that something is true, it exists, and you believe in it. Affirmations are a powerful tool in witchcraft as they serve as a constant reminder that there is a limitless power in your intent and belief – they are a kind of spell that you cast on yourself, and there is magick in every word! State who you want to be, or what you want to accomplish, or what you desire, as if it is already so. "I let go of the past", "I am respected", "I got the job" – such affirmations are the very beginnings of manifesting your desires.

Alchemy

The art of transformation or transmutation. The act of creating something extraordinary from the ordinary. In ancient times alchemists would attempt to make gold from lead, and though this term is sometimes still used, modern alchemists no longer focus on metals but will transform things in other way, such as using herbs to make medicinal potions, for example.

Alexandrian Witch

A witch who follows the teachings of Alex Sanders, who created his own tradition of the neo-pagan religion of Wicca, Alexandrian Wicca, in the United Kingdom in the 1960s.

Alomancy

Divination using salt. There are several ways to read salt, one is to take a handful of it, ask a question, and drop it onto a dark, flat surface or tray. Gaze at the salt and notice any symbols, swirls or patterns, and how these might relate or respond to the question posed. Alternatively, you can cast your salt into a fire, and read how the flames react, the patterns they form, the way they dance, etc. As with all divination, it is best not to try to force answers, so keep your mind relaxed and open, and remember that often you will 'sense' something, more than you can 'see' it.

✦ ✳ ✦

Altar

The ritual workspace – a table, shelf, or other dedicated area where witches practice their craft. For some witches altars can be a place where they cast regular spells, perform rituals and magickal workings, for others it is simply a sacred space where they place symbolic objects. There is nothing to suggest that a witch's altar should be dedicated to a specific religious path; indeed there are witches across all religions, and some witches worship nothing but Mother Earth. An altar can be a grand, elaborate table filled with ornate items and magickal tools, or it can be a simple candle on a shelf – the point being that it is a place that serves as a focal point for a witch's practice, and it should be only what they want it to be, nothing more, nothing less.

✦ ✳ ✦

Amulet

An object which has been ascribed magickal powers, or with which intentions have been set. In witchcraft, an amulet or talisman is a kind of 'good luck charm' imbued with the intention of the witch and then carried with them so they can draw from its energy when needed. Amulets are often added to charm bags or spell bottles to increase their potency, tied to door handles for protection or good fortune, or carried in the pocket or purse.

Angel Numbers

A sequence of numbers where all the numbers are the same, or predictable. Usually groups of three or four numbers, such as 111, or 4444, or numbers in sequence such as 3456. Those with a belief in numerology consider seeing angel numbers in random places such as a digital clock, a number plate, or a receipt, for example, is a sign from angels. Sometimes what you are feeling, thinking or doing at that moment is of significance, and the angels want you to pay attention. Sometimes the number is a simple reassuring sign that your angels are around. Or it could be that the number itself has a meaning that those who study numerology can decipher.

Angel Witch

A witch who works with angels. An angel witch will invoke the powers of angels to help them with their magick. Often angels are called upon for guidance and help in the same way some witches call upon deities.

Anoint

To sprinkle, rub or apply a liquid, usually as part of a ritual or ceremony. For example, in witchcraft, magickal tools and candles are anointed with potions or oils to match the witch's intentions and to infuse them with the magickal energy of the oil or potion used. If you are trying to attract something during your magick, anoint by rubbing the liquid onto the tool or candle towards yourself, if you are trying to banish, anoint by sweeping away from you.

Apparition

A supernatural presence that is visible to the eye, such as a ghost or phantom. An unexpected or unusual appearance of something paranormal. The more literal meaning is 'an appearance', so occasionally the word 'apparition' is used scientifically, such as in astronomy when a star becomes visible; but most often this word is used to describe a supernatural or inexplicable appearance.

Astral Travel
aka Astral Projection

Astral travel is where the soul leaves the physical body and enters the astral plane, where – while they can simply observe – some claim to encounter and interact with spiritual beings and entities during their travel. Unlike an involuntary 'out of body experience', astral travel involves an intentional effort to direct your soul from your body. Before attempting astral travel, it is recommended to research and learn as much about it as possible, or find an expert to take advice from to ensure it is practiced safely.

Astrology

A form of divination using the study and interpretation of the stars and planets. Astrologers study the celestial bodies, their movements and relative position, believing that these have an impact on, or influence over, our world here on earth. By looking at a person's astrological chart, which is created from their exact place and time of birth, a lot can be discovered about the person's personality, their past, present and future, and from this information guidance can be offered.

Athame

A ceremonial dagger, knife or blade (most commonly with a black handle and a double-edged blade) used to channel and direct energy and cast protective circles. Athames are often used to 'cut' energetic ties, but as the blade is not usually used for the cutting of physical objects, it is often beautiful rather than functional. To make a physical cut a different knife (or boline) is used. Unlike the gentle energy of a wand, the athame has a firm, commanding energy.

Aura

The atmosphere surrounding any given thing. All things have an aura, though it is generally more subtle in inanimate objects. The aura is an energy field which emanates from and surrounds the body. Thanks to the work of the writer and spiritual healer, Barbara Brennan, a former NASA physicist who studied the energy fields of the earth, it is thought that the aura has seven layers, and can reflect the health or emotional and spiritual wellbeing of a person. Some people claim to see or 'read' auras, and those who do, see them as a coloured light that radiates outwards from the body or object for a few inches to a few feet. It is said that a lot can be understood about a person by the colour of their aura. Sometimes you may feel that a person has a good or bad 'vibe' for no apparent reason, but it is likely that you are picking up on the person's aura, which is giving off a specific energetic vibration.

Casting a Magick Circle

✺

Before you begin your magickal workings, or perhaps before meditating, you may wish to surround yourself with an energy field.

You will need: athame or wand (optional, see *Athame* and *Wand*)

Since you cast it with the intent that only positive energies may be allowed to enter, the circle provides protection. Not only this, but it contains and amplifies your own personal energies making your magick more powerful.

There are many ways to cast a circle, and this is just one of them:

✷ Decide on a place to practice your magick where you won't be disturbed.

✷ Relax and breathe, ground and centre yourself.

✷ Stand in the centre of the circle, facing east.

✷ Imagine the wind all around you and tune in to the element of air.

✷ With an athame, wand or finger, draw the outline of a pentacle in mid-air – say:

"I call upon the energies of air."

✷ Continue to 'cast' the circle (clockwise) with your athame, wand or finger, until you face south. Imagine the fire crackling as you tune in to the element of fire.

RITUAL

* With an athame, wand or finger, draw the outline of a pentacle in mid-air – say:

"I call upon the energies of fire."

* Continue to 'cast' the circle (clockwise) with your athame, wand or finger, until you face west. Imagine rain and waves and the power of water all around as you tune in.

* With an athame, wand or finger, draw the outline of a pentacle in mid-air – say:

"I call upon the energies of water."

* Continue to 'cast' the circle (clockwise) with your athame, wand or finger, until you face north. Feel the earth under your feet and send invisible roots down through the soles of your feet to connect with the earth. With an athame, wand or finger, draw the outline of a pentacle in mid-air – say:

"I call upon the energies of earth."

* Now you can do your magickal work in the safety of your circle.

* When you've finished your work, thank the spirits individually by bringing them into your thoughts and acknowledging them (for example, "Air, thank you for being here", and so on).

* Before you step out of your circle say:

"The circle is open, but never broken."

You can now leave your magickal space.

Baby Witch

Often considered a derogatory term. A new, inexperienced witch; a newcomer to the craft, who has just started out on their journey and has had little practice. It is advised to only use the label 'baby witch' if it is self-applied and a label you wish to use; to apply it to someone else could be seen as offensive as it suggests a 'helplessness'. The word 'novice' or 'new' is preferable when referring to others, since these terms suggest an ability to move forward independently.

+ ✷ +

Balefire

An outdoor fire or ritualistic bonfire which, in witchcraft, is lit solely for magickal purposes. Traditionally balefires were constructed from bales of hay, and lit to celebrate a specific season or sabbat and keep evil spirits at bay. These days a variety of woods can be used in their construction – the choice of which can depend on the magickal properties of the wood, and the purpose of the fire. It is fairly common for witches and pagans to dance around or jump over the fire as they believe it to have protective properties. When the fire dies down, the ashes can be collected for use in magickal workings to do with protection or fertility.

As always when working with fire, safety is of paramount importance, and just because something's become a part of a tradition, that doesn't mean it's safe! I encourage you dance at a safe distance from the flames in case you should stumble – and personally, I do not recommend jumping over the balefire.

+ ✷ +

Banishing

To remove something, to make it go away. In magick we often focus on banishing stagnant or negative energies or spirits, and banishing spells are often performed to clear the space of negativity before any other magick takes place. Banishing spells can also be used to banish other things in our lives such as gossip, or even to ward off unpleasant people.

Beltane

aka Beltaine or Bealtaine

One of the eight sabbats, Beltane is an ancient fertility festival; a joyous event marking the beginning of the planting cycle, ensuring a bountiful harvest. Rituals for abundance are appropriate at this time, as is time spent outdoors.

+ ✵ +

Besom

A traditional broomstick made of twigs tied to a sturdy pole. It is customary for the handle to be of hazel or ash with twigs of birch, though witches often craft their brooms with materials to match their intentions. Large besoms are used to sweep the home, or remove negative or stagnant energy from a ritual space. As this is a spiritual or metaphorical cleaning, in many traditions the besom does not touch the ground but is used just above it. Small besoms can be used to clear the altar in the same way, sweeping counter-clockwise to clear away negativity. Store a besom bristles up to attract good fortune, or stand it by the door to protect the home.

+ ✵ +

Bewitch

To exert power over someone or something by magickal means. To use magick to make someone feel, think or behave in a particular way. A person may be considered 'bewitching' on account of their beauty or charisma, but in witchcraft to bewitch is a deliberate magickal act.

+ ✵ +

Binding

A spell that restrains someone and prevents them from feeling or behaving a certain way. A binding spell may be used to prevent an individual from causing harm to themselves or others, or to bind two people together in a love spell. Binding spells are controversial because, by nature, they cause someone to think or act against their own will and, in the case of love spells, could result in two people being compelled to stay together even though one or both of them is unhappy.

Black Magick

Magick used for evil or selfish purposes. Spells and rituals performed maliciously and with ill-intent. Very controversial.

Black Salt

A protective salt for use in spells and rituals for protection, banishing or hex-breaking. Many witches create their own black salt by saving the ashes from incense, or burning protective herbs and stirring the ashes into white salt to colour it black and add protective energy.

There are many magickal uses for black salt. As well as being used to dress candles, or as an addition to spell jars (to name just a few applications), this salt can be sprinkled across thresholds and windowsills to keep negative energies from entering, or used to make a protective circle for working magick. Walking counter-clockwise and sprinkling the salt around the boundary of the home is one way to protect the home from negative energy. The list of uses for this magickal salt is endless.

Blessed Be

A Wiccan greeting. A way of wishing someone blessings, happiness and good fortune.

Boline

Also spelled 'bolline' or 'bolleen'. A boline is a white-handled knife which, unlike the athame, is used for practical work before or during spells and rituals, such as cutting herbs, cords, wands etc, or inscribing candles. The boline sometimes has a small, straight blade, but a crescent-shaped blade is not uncommon.

Book of Shadows

A book of instructions for magickal rituals and spells. Often also containing religious text and personal thoughts, the Book of Shadows was at first associated with the Wiccan religion, although Books of Shadows are now widely used by witches of all religious paths. Unlike a grimoire, a Book of Shadows has more of a 'journal' quality, since it is often used for recording experiences and emotions, rather than just ingredients and instructions.

Botanical

Relating to plants. The word 'botanical' can be used to refer to any plants, herb, flower etc that we use in our craft.

Botanomancy

Divination using plants. Perhaps one of the most often-used forms of divination since most of us, even as children, have pulled the petals from a daisy and said "he loves me, he loves me not" with the final petal giving us the answer (you can use this for any yes/no question). This is a perfect example of botanomancy. Another method is to peel an apple so that the peel comes off in one long strip, ask a question, then toss it over your left shoulder – look for an answer in the shape it forms on the floor behind you. Herbs can be tossed into a fire so the flames and smoke can be read and interpreted, and answers can be heard in the crackles and hisses of the fire. Branches can be burned, the smoke can be read, as can the ashes the fire has left behind. As you can see, there are countless ways to seek answers through plants, and these are just a few examples.

Self-Love Charm Bag

✴

Here's a simple charm bag to encourage you to love yourself. I hope this magickal pouch will remind you treat yourself with the kindness you deserve.

You will need: jasmine flowers, marjoram, poppy seeds, a drawstring pouch (preferably pink or white), a rose quartz crystal

✴ Blend the herbs together in a clockwise motion to attract self-love and as you do so, consider all the beautiful qualities you possess. Imagine you are your own best friend and be kind with your thoughts. Imbue the herbs with your gentle, loving energy.

State the following:

"Self-love and appreciation shall come to me
As I will it, so mote it be."

✴ Sit with the rose quartz in your hand and feel its loving vibration filling you up.

✴ Know that love is engulfing you, surrounding you.

✴ Visualise a soft pink light rising up through you, out of you, and surrounding you in its loving embrace.

✴ Feel the emotion of love – this love is pure and it's for you!

✴ Add the herb blend and rose quartz to the pouch and tie it firmly closed.

✴ Keep this bag close by, and draw from its loving energy when needed.

Candle Magick

A kind of magick incorporating candles. Anyone who has ever blown out the candles on their birthday cake and made a wish has practiced candle magick! It can be as simple as that, but more often candles are carved with sigils to represent intent, and dressed in oils, herbs or crystal chips before they are lit. As the candle burns, intentions are reaffirmed, outcomes are visualised and gratitude given. For safety, choose what you anoint and dress your candle with carefully, and never leave a lit candle unattended.

Candle magick can stand alone, or be a part of an elaborate ritual, or a simple meditation, such as this:

Once you have set your intention, choose the perfect coloured candle to match it. Anoint or dress your candle in a way that feels right to you, then visualise your desires becoming a reality. Light the candle when you are feeling full of joy and gratitude for that positive outcome.

Once the candle is lit, focus on the aura from the flame and visualise it growing, expanding and becoming limitless, like a beacon sharing your desires with the universe. You should allow the candle to burn all the way down, but if at any point you feel your energy dipping, it's time to snuff out the candle with gratitude (don't blow it out, since this can dissipate the energy of the spell).

Whether you light a plain candle or anoint and dress a specific one, so long as your intention is there, and you believe and visualise the outcome, there is power in your craft.

Cartomancy

A form of fortune-telling or divination which traditionally uses a deck of regular playing cards. Playing cards were first invented in Europe in the 14th century, and it was soon after that cartomancy was practiced. Similar to a tarot deck, each card in the deck has its own meaning. Unlike tarot, the cards are much more precise in their meaning, and so rely less on the intuition of the reader – though it's fair to say that those with heightened intuition may be able to reveal more in-depth messages by reading the connections between one card turned and the next.

Catoptromancy

aka Mirror Scrying

Catoptromancy is a form of divination. There are several forms of catoptromancy, but here's an example of scrying with a clear glass mirror, since this is something which most people will have readily available.

Mirror scrying with a clear glass mirror:

This is best done in semi-darkness, ideally with just the glow from the moon gently illuminating the space. It is best to position your mirror so nothing directly reflects in it, arrange candles around the mirror in a way that casts both light and shade across the mirror. You can also experiment with burning incense on either side of the mirror to help create a more 'fluid' doorway into the mirror. Recommended incenses are lavender, patchouli and rosemary, since these are believed to enhance psychic abilities and aid divination.

Gaze into the mirror. Ask your question, and repeat it getting quieter and quieter each time until it is barely a whisper. Blink slowly and gaze deep into the mirror. See what image presents itself. You must interpret what you've seen by using your instinct, your intuition.

When you are ready to ask another question, turn your palm towards the mirror and wave in a counter-clockwise sweeping circle to clear the past images, this can also be achieved by blowing gently on the surface of the mirror. Give thanks to the mirror for sharing its wisdom, then continue.

Cauldron

A pot which was traditionally made of metal, had a lid and a handle, and was used for cooking and boiling over an open fire. The cauldron is associated with (and often placed on the altar to represent) the divine feminine. While the classic imagery of a cauldron shows it bubbling magickal concoctions over leaping flames, today the cauldron is more often a smaller, more understated fireproof pot which is used to burn herbs and incense, brew herbal potions and cast fire magick spells etc.

Celtic Witch

A witch who observes the ancient Celtic traditions. Celtic witchcraft worships the rhythm and energies of the Earth and celebrates them with four major Celtic festivals (Imbolc, Beltane, Lughnasadh and Samhain). Celtic witches work in harmony with the natural world and the changes of the seasons, and believe that everything is connected and that everything, including the wind, trees, lakes etc, has a spirit energy. It is this energy that they tap into for their magick. Ancestral work is common, with ancestors being called upon for wisdom, guidance and protection.

Centering

Centering is performed after grounding and is the process of drawing all of the energy inside and around you together so you can channel it into your spell work. You can do this by focusing on the scattered energy that you feel within and around you, visualising those energies rolling together like liquid metal or water droplets, connecting and coming together in a pool, which turns into a ball of powerful, focused energy that you have control over. You can align this energy with your intention and use it during your magickal workings. Once your spell work is completed, you can rid yourself of this intense energy by grounding yourself and releasing it into the earth.

Ceremonial Witch

A ceremonial witch will practice elaborate ceremonies, rituals and spells. Their magick will have an emphasis on exact ceremonial procedures, symbolism and structure. They will go through specific steps, actions and dialogue when working their magick, and they often follow ancient traditions. They will use tools such as wands and athames to help them to focus and direct their energy. And through their magickal ceremonies and rituals they can achieve a higher state of consciousness.

Ceromancy

aka Carromancy

This is a form of divination using wax. There are two main ways of wax scrying.

For candle ceromancy:

Use an ordinary plain candle to observe both the movement and actions of the flame, and also of the wax as it becomes molten and drips down the side of the candle and/or candle holder. It is necessary for this method to use a candle which will drip. Non-drip candles will reveal very little since their wax will not flow.

Light your candle, and as you do this you may ask any question you would like to have answered, or else you may simply welcome any and all messages which may appear.

Watch the flame as it flickers and dances, does it hold a message for you? Or perhaps the message will be revealed in the wax as it turns to liquid and bleeds down the sides of the candle. Gaze into the movement, and remember that scrying is not only a visual art, but a spiritual one too so be open to your feelings and intuition, and the answers and/or messages will present themselves.

For ceromancy using water:

The second common method of ceromancy is to drip molten wax into water and to look at the shapes that are subsequently formed in both the wax and the water as they swirl together, and in the hardened wax as it solidifies and floats on the surface of the water.

For this method, it is preferable to choose a through-coloured candle, since many candles are only dipped in coloured wax and are actually white under their coloured surface. This white wax does not contrast with the water nearly so much as a darker colour, and can therefore yield unsatisfactory results. For those new to the art, darker blues and purples can give the clearest images. Though it is also thought useful to select an appropriate candle colour if your questions are all going to relate to a specific topic; for example, pink for love and relationships, green for finances etc.

Once you feel more practised in the art of wax scrying, you may wish to add in more candles, and multiple colours.

Half fill a bowl with water and light your candle. Relax and allow your gaze to shift from the flame to the surface of the water and back again, to build a relationship between the fire and the water. At this stage you may want to ask a specific question, or else leave it open and allow any messages which are meant for you to come through.

Take your candle in your dominant hand and begin to drip the wax in a circular motion from the centre outwards (as you are requesting that answers come to you, drip the wax clockwise to invoke). Then watch as your message appears. Note not only the appearance of the wax but also the ripples and shadows which appear on the water, use your intuition to decipher what you see.

On an occasion where you feel nothing has been revealed, it can be beneficial to carefully lift the hardened wax from the bowl and set it aside to study later.

Chakras

Chakras are the energy centres in the body, which are believed to be like spinning disks of energy that should be kept open and aligned for our spiritual and physical wellbeing. While chakras have their roots in India and Hinduism, there is no doubt that many witches from all religions work with chakras. There are seven major chakras in the human body, as follows:

ROOT CHAKRA

Colour: Red

Location: Base of the spine

Stability, identity, self, trust, grounding

SACRAL CHAKRA

Colour: Orange

Location: Above the pubic bone, below the belly button

Creativity, sexuality, pleasure

SOLAR PLEXUS CHAKRA

Colour: Yellow

Location: Stomach/upper abdomen

Confidence, personality, self esteem

HEART CHAKRA

Colour: Green

Location: The centre of the chest

Compassion, empathy, love, forgiveness

THROAT CHAKRA

Colour: Blue

Location: The throat

Communication, expression

THIRD EYE CHAKRA

Colour: Indigo/purple

Location: On the forehead, in the centre, just above the eyes

Imagination, intuition, psychic awareness

CROWN CHAKRA

Colour: Violet or white

Location: Top of the head

Enlightenment, awareness, spirituality

If your chakras become blocked or sluggish you may feel physical tension and negative emotions that may feel out of your control. There are crystals that are associated with each chakra, and placing these at the corresponding point on your body can help to bring balance and to open your chakras. Reiki (an ancient energy-healing practice which works with the flow of energy in the body) is also a recognised treatment for blocked chakras.

Chalice

A drinking vessel intended for ceremonial drinking. Often used to represent the element of water on a witch's altar, it is also a symbol of femininity and fertility. It is traditional in many covens to pass the chalice around for each coven member to take a sip to symbolise their bond. Witches who work with deities will use their chalice for liquid offerings.

Channeling

Using energy and/or power from another source. This is done by connecting with a spirit, deity, element or other non-physical entity to gain wisdom, or to draw from its energy and channel that into your magickal workings.

Chant

A chant is a rhythmic sound or set of words, which are often repeated during spells and rituals to build energy and add strength to a spell. The purpose of a chant is to set intentions and raise vibrations during magickal workings.

Chaos Magick

An experimental magick. Chaos magick isn't a tangible kind of magick, it is more an attitude. A witch or practitioner who claims to practice chaos magick will explore a vast variety of traditions, cultures and practices; they will cast aside any that they don't find effective, and find the most productive way for them to practice their craft. The practitioner believes in their own magickal practice, which is eclectic in nature, but does not believe that any one idea or rule can apply to all people, or even a group of people.

+ ✶ +

Charge

The act of bringing your energy and power to an object in order to give it purpose. This is a very important part of most witches' magickal practice. Objects have their own unique power, but you can also charge them with your own energy and intentions. A very simple example would be to take a wooden spoon, hold it in your hand, and charge it with your own healing energy with intent that whatever the spoon stirs, will promote healing. To do this you visualise the energy transferring from you into the spoon, you expect the desired outcome, and feel gratitude for it. Your energy, intent and belief are where the magick lies. Then, as you stir your soup, for example, the healing energy will transfer into the food and whoever consumes it will benefit from its healing properties. Crystals, amulets and jewellery are commonly charged items, but you can charge any item at all in this way.

+ ✶ +

Charm

A charm is magickal object which attracts a desired outcome. Anything can be a charm, from a piece of jewellery to a coin, a crystal, a flower etc. The thing that makes a charm a charm is that it has been charged with a particular intention in mind. By charging the item with your energy and intent, it becomes a magickal, enchanted charm, created in order to attract a successful outcome.

Charm Bag

aka Conjure Bag/Mojo Bag

A magickal bag filled with things that represent your intention, with the purpose of achieving a pre-determined outcome. Typically, the pouch is filled with herbs, crystals, affirmations, amulets etc, which have been charged with your intention, and then (depending on its intended use) kept in your home, on your altar, or carried with you. You can sit with your charm bag from time to time to reaffirm your intention and recharge it. Once you feel that the charm bag no longer serves, any herbs can be offered back to the earth with thanks, and crystals can be cleansed for re-use.

Clairvoyant

Someone with extrasensory perception. Clairvoyants have the ability to see the future, or other things which are beyond the scope of ordinary perception. Clairvoyants often claim to communicate with the dead, or to be able to tell the history of an object simply by touching it. Some can sense what has happened in a room, simply by entering it. The clairvoyant has a special ability to see, hear and sense the supernatural.

Cleansing

The act of ridding a space, object or person of negative, unwanted or stagnant energy. One of the most common methods of cleansing a space or a person is smoke cleansing, but there are other approaches such as the ringing of bells. When cleansing objects rather than a space, burying them for a while in salt or earth is a common cleansing method, or cleansing using moonlight or sunlight, and of course water; though if you are cleansing crystals, be mindful that some can be damaged if they get wet.

Conjure

To cause something to appear by magickal means; to summon by invocation or by incantation. This word was historically used when referring to summoning a spirit or other supernatural entity. This term should not be confused with the slight-of-hand illusions of stage magic.

+ ✷ +

Cord Cutting

A spell to cut ties with a person, situation or emotion. If you feel somehow tied to a negative relationship, bad habit, a person, situation or emotion that is draining and no longer serves you, a cord cutting ritual may be able to help. Sometimes we connect energetically with things, addictions and people. A cord cutting is a magickal ritual that can help you to disconnect and sever the ties that are holding you back. This can help to banish fear, and release attachment and resentment, so you can move on with your life unshackled. If you need help to energetically detach yourself from someone or something, so that you can be empowered to move on, then this ritual can help you. A cord cutting ritual should be done with no malice to anyone. Your intention here should never be harm, only to sever ties.

One simple cord cutting is as follows:

Stand two black candles on a fireproof tray, a couple of inches apart. Tie them together with string. Do this with the intention that one candle represents you and the other represents the person/emotion/thing you are separating yourself from.

Light the candles and state the following:

"As the cord is cut and the candles burned,
I cut all ties with that for which I yearned,
I release what no longer serves me,
As I will it, so mote it be."

Sit and meditate as the candles burn and the cord is cut by the flame. Visualise your energetic attachment to the person/emotion/thing being cut. Feel yourself becoming detached, empowered and able to move on without this in your life.

Cosmic Witch

A witch who incorporates celestial bodies and their movements into their craft. While most witches work with the cycles of the moon and lunar energy, a cosmic witch includes many aspects of astrology and astronomy, and will use not only the power of the moon in their magick, but also the power of celestial events. A cosmic witch will work with moon phases, but will also pay attention to what zodiac sign the moon is in, and work their magick accordingly.

Coven

A gathering of at least three witches who come together to discuss witchcraft, learn together, teach each other, practice their craft, and pass down any traditions of their coven. Because their magick is amplified by the number of witches involved, by using their collective energy they can often cast powerful magick. Covens are often (but not always) led by a High Priestess, a High Priest, or both. Covens will gather, usually in nature, to celebrate the sabbats, for rituals, initiations etc. It is wise to avoid taking part in initiations which make you feel uncomfortable, or to pay to be a part of a coven. Often, each member of a coven will specialise in a particular kind of magick, such as divination or healing, which means that the coven as a whole has a well-rounded knowledge and skillset.

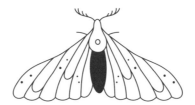

Craft

The craft is an abbreviation of 'witchcraft', and is how many witches refer to their own individual practice. An appropriate word, since witchcraft is a practice in which we are always learning, acquiring new skills, growing our abilities, honing our power, and therefore honing our very own, unique craft.

Crone

Many Wiccan traditions honour the Triple Goddess, and each aspect of the Goddess represents a different stage in a woman's life. The crone is associated with the latter stage of life, great wisdom, life-experience, resilience, spiritual awareness and reflection. Rituals invoking the crone are performed during the waning moon or the new moon.

Often considered an insult to those outside of the magickal community, to many pagans and Wiccans 'crone' is an honorific! 'Crone' is an earned status in which they take great pride. Many will even hold a 'croning' – a ceremony to celebrate this important transition. Most croning ceremonies take place when the subject is over the age of fifty, and some traditions' guidelines are that a woman should be through the menopause before her croning. It is a time to honour the wisdom earned through decades of experience and learning.

Crystal Ball

A spherical shaped crystal used for divination. While all crystals can be used for scrying, the clear quartz crystal ball is the most traditional. The most important thing is to select a ball which you feel a connection to. Whatever you choose, the benefit of crystal over clear glass is that crystal has natural fractures and formations which allow your gaze to shift into both the shallows and the deep.

It is best to have some kind of light at play, whether this be candle light, sunlight or moonlight. Attune to your ball's energies by cupping her in your hands, bonding with her through your delicate palms and sensitive fingertips; feel her energy, and develop a personal connection with her.

Using a crystal ball:

Position the ball so that the light source brings the ball to life. Relax your gaze and open your mind to the images and symbols that begin to form – you may be surprised at just how much detail presents itself. As you study the images, they may transform into others; be mindful of how these images may relate to one another. It is sensible, when starting out with a crystal ball, to journal what you see, as you may need to study this later in order to see how the images relate to the questions asked, and to each other. In time, you will know intuitively.

If you can't see anything of note. Gaze right into the centre of the ball intensely, hold your gaze until you feel your eyes closing. Slowly open your eyes and look into the ball again, perhaps a vision will present itself now. Sometimes you will 'sense' an image, more than you can 'see' it. Pay mind to this – your connection with your ball is more than just visual.

Crystal Grid

A crystal grid is a special geometric arrangement of crystals with a set intention. The grid is created to amplify the power of the crystals and to combine the powers of multiple crystals towards one end goal. There are many ways of working with grids, and the following is a very simplified description of just one of those methods:

The choice of grid patterns you can use is endless, so feel free to be creative! Your main crystal (the largest of the crystals you are working with) is placed in the centre, with your smaller crystals laid in a geometric pattern around the main crystal.

Next place one finger of your dominant hand on the centre crystal and focus your intent. Move your finger around each of the crystals connecting their energies while setting your intent and activating your grid.

Meditate on your desired outcome and leave the grid in place for as long as is needed. Go back every few days to connect the energies, meditate and re-focus your intent.

✦ ✶ ✦

Crystal Healing

An alternative or complementary therapy, crystal healing uses crystals to bring harmony and healing to the human body and mind. This is an energy-based therapy that draws on the unique vibration of each crystal to bring fresh energy, and help us balance and unblock our own energy centres (chakras) in the body. Each crystal has its own unique vibration and energy, and each cell in the human body also has its own energy. When a crystal is brought close to the body, sensitive people can feel the energies from the crystal, which can help to bring their own energy into balance. Choosing the right crystal is simple; you hold one in your hand and see if your energy shifts, and whether you start to feel a connection to that crystal. While some crystals are believed to be helpful with certain issues or ailments, there should be no hard and fast rules. Choose the ones that resonate with your own energy and feel right to you.

Crystal Magick

All crystals have their own natural properties that you can draw on, which means they are excellent additions to charm bags and spell jars etc. It is recommended that you set your own intentions to get the most out of the magickal energies in your crystals.

Here's how to charge a crystal with your intent:

Choose a crystal which feels right to you and is appropriate for what you'd like to achieve (it could be rose quartz for love, amethyst for health, citrine for abundance etc).

Find a time when you can be completely at peace, and with your mind free from any negativity, hold the crystal in the palm of your hand. Feel a connection to the crystal and imagine a white light emanating from it and surrounding you completely. Once you feel fully connected to your crystal, meditate on your intention, see what you desire as if it were already realised. Continue until you feel your intention is set.

Once your intention is set, you can use this crystal in your spellcraft, or simply keep the crystal close by, in which case, it's very helpful to keep it within your auric field as much as possible, so try sleeping with it under your pillow or keeping it in your pocket.

Reset your intentions at regular intervals to remain connected to your crystal.

Different shapes and forms of crystals work in different ways. Here are some examples:

TUMBLED STONES

The smooth, rounded shape of tumbled stones makes them ideal for carrying with us in our pockets or in our clothing, and they can be easily tucked away in our car or on our desk etc. A relatively inexpensive form of crystal, tumbled stones are usually where we first begin our crystal journey.

CRYSTAL POINTS

Crystals which come to a natural point at one end. These are powerful manifestation tools. Crystal points can be used to direct energy into the universe, in rituals, or in crystal healing.

CRYSTAL TOWERS

Crystal towers are crystals that have been shaped into a point and are also flat on one end, allowing them to stand. These can be used in much the same way as crystal points.

CRYSTAL CLUSTERS

A crystal cluster is formed by several crystal points growing together. This causes a higher vibration of energy to be directed in multiple directions. Crystal clusters are not only stunningly beautiful, but adding one to your space will ensure the entire room in which it is benefits from its energy!

SPHERES

Emitting energy in all directions, a crystal sphere brings great balance to its surroundings. There is a sense of wholeness that comes from meditating with spheres as they connect you fully with the universal energy surrounding you.

PYRAMIDS

While the base of these crystals anchors your intention, the apex of the pyramid sends it out into the universe – there is no more powerful crystal shape to amplify your intentions and manifest your desires.

Crystal Witch

A witch who specialises in working with crystals. Crystal witches work with the unique vibrations of crystals and use them to raise their own vibration, and to focus their own energy while performing their magick. They will wear crystal jewellery, use crystals as amulets, add them to their spell jars and charm bags, sleep with them under their pillow, and even drink water imbued with crystal magick. They are often healers and can be very adept at crystal healing.

Curse

A pronouncement of ill-fortune. A call for harm, misfortune or injury. Spoken words with the power to bring about bad luck. Unlike a spell intended to cause harm, a curse requires nothing other than focused intent and the spoken word. A witch's energy and harmful intent, combined with words, are all it takes to cast a curse, and witches should be mindful of this power.

Cyclomancy

A form of divination using a spinning object. Insight and predictions are derived from the way the object spins and moves, and from where and how it comes to rest. Often some kind of board or cloth with special sigils, words or letters is used to help the reader to decipher the message.

Distance Healing Spell Powder

✶

There will be times when you wish to heal someone who isn't present – a healing powder is the ideal way to send healing energies their way.

You will need: fennel seeds, barley, rosemary, rue

- ✶ Grind your herbs down into a fine powder, do this clockwise with the intent to attract healing.
- ✶ Think about the person you are wishing to heal – imagine them on the mend and feeling better.
- ✶ Take your powder outdoors in the palm of your hand, and state the following:

**"I call upon the element of air
To carry healing with loving care,
I send my healing energy with thee,
As I will it, so mote it be."**

- ✶ Holding the person you are healing in your mind with love and kindness, and visualising them feeling better, blow your spell powder in the direction of the person you are hoping to heal. It doesn't matter if this person is thousands of miles away, you are setting your intention to heal with the act of blowing.
- ✶ Thank the elements of earth and air for helping you with your magick.

Your spell is complete.

Deity

A God or Goddess or other divine supernatural being.

While the primary Wiccan deities are the feminine and masculine aspects of the Divine – the Triple Goddess (feminine) and the Horned God (masculine) – there are many other pagan Gods and Goddesses that are worshipped and called upon by witches. There are witches across all religions, and while some worship one God or Goddess, others worship several.

Deosil

Other accepted spellings: deasil, deiseal, deisal or deisul. This means clockwise or sunwise, and in witchcraft is used to attract or bring things to you. For example, when stirring a love potion, you would stir it clockwise to attract love. If making an abundance charm bag, blend the contents clockwise to attract money, and so on.

Dianic Witch

Witches who follow the Dianic tradition honour and worship the Goddess Diana.

Dianic witchcraft has feminist values and a heavy focus on the empowerment of women. It holds to a belief system that values women, and aims to deconstruct the religious and societal beliefs of the patriarchy.

Divination

Divination is the practice of seeking knowledge of the future, or the unknown, by using your own intuition and insight in order to translate the images, visions or messages that come through your chosen divination tool. Divination is not just about 'fortune telling', it is a means to find answers to questions posed by the querent and give advice based on what is seen. There is an art to divination, and it is true that many people seem to have a natural gift, but this is also something that can be mastered over time as you learn to tune into your intuition.

Where the quested-for knowledge comes from is a mystery; some believe the messages are from a deity, others believe they are from spirit guides, or angels, or 'the universe'... Wherever they come from, when used properly they can give us useful insight.

It is important to realise that when working with questions about the future, the diviner is predicting the probable outcome based on the forces that are currently at play. This means that the querent can use the insights they receive for guidance and, should they not like what they hear, they can change their path and alter their outcome. So free will is always there for us to use, and any insight we can have into the path we are on can be useful.

If working with a querent, it is important to speak the truth with kindness. The goal should be to bring hope, inspiration and healing. You should never thoughtlessly deal someone a hammer-blow that you feel will cause damage.

Dowsing

Dowsing is a method of detecting water, minerals or other hidden objects, using a Y-shaped piece of wood, or metal rod. In witchcraft, a dowsing pendulum is also often used; this is a metal, wooden or crystal pendulum hanging from a chain or cord. Not only are these used to locate hidden items, but also as a divination tool to give insight into the unknown. Answers are found by the direction the pendulum swings, and sometimes with the aid of a pendulum board or cloth.

— ✦ ✶ ✦

Drawing Down the Moon

aka Drawing Down the Goddess

This is an important ritual in many modern Wiccan traditions in which the practitioner (usually the High Priestess of the coven) enters a trance-like state, and invokes the Goddess (symbolised by the moon), that the Goddess may use her body as a vessel and speak through her. There is more than one way to 'Draw Down the Moon', depending on differing traditions, and it is important to be well-prepared beforehand, as it is a powerful, and often emotional and exhausting ritual.

— ✦ ✶ ✦

Dressing Candles

Coating a candle in magickal oils, herbs, spell powders or crystal chips to prepare it for a spell or ritual. This can be done by coating the candle in oil, or lightly melting the surface with a flame and then rolling it in appropriate herbs, spell powders or crystals chips while the surface is still semi-liquid.

— ✦ ✶ ✦

Druid

A practitioner of modern Druidry (or Druidism). Druids worship the natural world. They don't necessarily identify as witches or Wiccan (though some do), but they share many beliefs and often socialise together, as do pagans from many religions.

Eclectic Witch

A witch who takes knowledge from anywhere and everywhere and practices witchcraft in a uniquely individual way. An eclectic witch is not bound by any rules or religion, but will follow whatever path works for them, taking what they need from other practices, beliefs and traditions to create their own personal way of practicing.

Egg Cleanse

Removing the negative energy from a person using an egg. An egg cleanse is performed by rolling an egg over the body of the subject so that it can absorb any negative energy they are harbouring. The egg is then cracked into a glass or bowl of water and 'read' to determine if the cleanse was successful.

Elements

Everything here in our physical world is made up of earth, air, fire and water. And the fifth element, spirit, is the binding force between all other elements, and between everything in existence. For hundreds, if not thousands of years, alchemists, witches and the like, have incorporated the powers and attributes of the four elements of the universe into their magick; and many also include the fifth element, spirit, into their magickal practices.

These five elements are essential to sustain life – they connect all things. There is a powerful flow of energy between them, and this energy is often called upon during magickal practices to add power to spells and rituals.

Elixir

A magickal or medicinal potion, a drinkable spell, a liquid concoction with the power to heal or preserve. Incorporating the magickal properties of an amalgamation of herbs and/or crystals in a liquid (often alcohol) base, an elixir is made with the purpose of affecting the body, spirit or mental health of the person who consumes it. The making of elixirs must be taken very seriously since many plants are poisonous and some crystals are toxic, so there could be severe health implications if the wrong concoction is used.

Empath

A person who senses what others are thinking and feeling. Empaths have the ability to tune into the emotions and feelings of others (often involuntarily), and are so sensitive to those emotions that they literally feel them as if they were their own. Empaths are very emotionally intelligent, and tend to be generous, caring and open-hearted. However they have a tendency to shoulder the burden of other people's problems, and can find it almost impossible to set boundaries. Being burdened with the emotions of others, and taking on the problems of others, can leave empaths feeling overwhelmed at times. Empaths can find social situations can trigger anxiety because they know that being around a lot of people, with so many different emotions, is likely to be draining, so it is essential that they regularly have time to be alone and recharge.

Enchant

To cast a spell on someone or something to make it behave in a specific way. Enchanting a person involves casting a spell on them to influence them in some way. Enchanting an object is to imbue the object with magickal energy and your own intentions, to give the object magickal properties.

Energy

According to physics, everything is energy! Energy is the building block for all matter; quantum physicists now recognise that even physical atoms, are made from vortices of energy which constantly vibrate and spin. It is this energy that runs through and connects everything that witches harness and work with to affect change and manifest their desired outcome.

Equinox

The two times in the year when there are an equal number of daylight and night-time hours. The March equinox occurs between the 19th and 21st of March (known as the Spring equinox in the northern hemisphere and the Autumn equinox in the southern hemisphere). The September equinox occurs between the 21st and 24th of September (known as the Autumn equinox in the northern hemisphere and the Spring equinox in the southern hemisphere).

During the Spring equinox witches focus on balance, rebirth, and new beginnings. This is a great time for purification spells, and spells for fresh starts or new projects.

During the Autumn equinox witches celebrate the fruits of their labour, and honour mother earth, giving thanks for her bounty. This is a time for walks in nature, for foraging and outdoor magick.

Esbat

A meeting of a coven of witches at a time other than one of the eight sabbats. Often these meetings are held once every moon cycle, usually during the full moon, and incorporate healing work, psychic and magickal training, moon rituals and initiations etc. Solitary witches who take advantage of the moon phases will often refer to their moon magick or rituals as 'esbats'.

Esoteric

Mysterious, unusual and unlikely to be understood or appreciated by anyone without specialised knowledge.

Evil Eye (The)

A curse brought about by a malevolent stare, glower, or glance, usually as a result of envy, and not always on purpose or consciously. Belief in misfortune as a result of being given 'the evil eye' has been around in many cultures for centuries, seemingly pre-dating the history books. Amulets created to ward of such misfortune exist among many cultures too. While some of these talismans have become very popular, in some cases their use could be considered to be cultural appropriation.

Evoke

To bring or call forth something intangible, such as a memory, feeling or emotion. In witchcraft, the word 'evoke' is often used when calling upon a deity. There is sometimes confusion between the word 'evoke' and 'invoke'. For clarity, when you 'evoke' something (such as a spirit or deity) you are simply inviting it to attend, you are asking for its presence; whereas 'invoke' is a calling *in* to something, either into your auric field, your mind, your body or a vessel.

Exorcism

The spiritual practice of driving out demons, negative spirits or other unwanted supernatural entities from a person or place which has been possessed. This is different to 'banishing', which deals with residual or negative energy. An exorcism deals with a spirit or entity, and expelling such evil from a person or place can be a very risky undertaking.

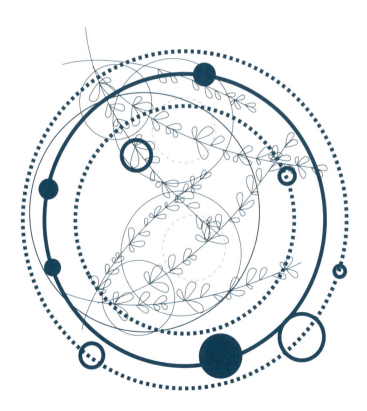

Familiar

Familiars are a witch's helpful, guardian spirits. Familiars may take the form of a pet, a spirit animal, or even an obliging non-physical entity. Not every witch has a familiar, and not all witches who have a familiar are aware of it, so watch out for animals with which you share a special bond, and if you desire it, work on that psychic connection. You may also find your familiar in the spiritual realm during meditation or astral travel.

Folk Witch

A witch who follows the path of, and practices the folk magic of, their ancestors and others from the same village or local community. Generally folk witches will be knowledgeable about local traditions and folklore, and may use the same spells and herbal recipes that have been used for generations.

Forest Witch

aka Garden Witch or Green Witch

A witch who works primarily in nature, and who incorporates many natural, earthly elements into their craft. A forest witch will practice their most powerful magick outdoors, connecting with the earth. They will often grow their own herbs, and study the flora and fauna in their local area to see how it can be used in their magickal workings.

Fortune Teller

A person with the ability to foretell future events. Usually specialising in a particular form of divination, such as palmistry, tea-leaf reading, tarot cards, crystal ball etc. Fortune tellers use their intuition and insight to translate the information that comes through in order to predict what will happen, give advice, or to answer specific questions the querent may pose.

Gardnerian Witch

A witch who follows Gardnerian Wicca. This tradition was created by Gerald Gardner in the 1950s. Gardner claimed to have been initiated into the New Forest Coven in 1939, and later incorporated many of their beliefs and practices into his own tradition, which is generally regarded as the earliest form of Wicca, from which all other Wiccan traditions are derived.

— ✦ ✴ ✦

Glamour Magick

A magickal working or spell that can change either the witch's appearance, or at least the way others perceive them. These days, glamour magick is not so much about conforming to beauty standards, or trying to be accepted for our physical appearance, but more often it's performing magick to make ourselves (and those around us) appreciate our true beauty, and our value. It's all about self-expression and amplifying our own unique energy to make ourselves magnetising, charismatic and powerful. This can be a spell as simple as setting an intention while putting on lipstick, for example: "every word that passes these lips today will be heard".

— ✦ ✴ ✦

Green Man (The)

Commonly depicted as a male face surrounded by leaves and foliage, the Green Man can be found as a decorative carving on many ancient buildings, from different cultures and time periods. In modern paganism, the Green Man is a symbol of nature, growth and rebirth. Some worship him as a deity, a god of the woodlands; to others he is not a deity, but a beautiful reminder of man's connection to nature.

Grimoire

A book of spells, rituals and magickal instructions. Traditionally a grimoire is a book containing only tried and trusted magickal directions, spells, incantations and invocations. It holds full instructions on how to prepare magickal tools and perform the spells and rituals within it. Unlike the more modern Book of Shadows, which contains writings about experiences, and emotions, and religious text, the grimoire is traditionally more of a magickal instruction book.

Grounding

The act of connecting yourself to the energies of the earth. Grounding is a way of releasing negative energy and stress, and restoring positive energy, to leave you feeling calmer and more focused. Once you are grounded, you can centre and use the powerful energy you have drawn from the earth in your magickal workings.

Here is a simple grounding technique:

This is best done outdoors, in nature and barefoot, but can be done anywhere, whenever you feel you need it.

Stand with the soles of your feet firmly on the ground.

Visualise 'roots' sprouting from the soles of your feet and reaching deep into the earth below.

Imagine these 'roots' reaching down into the earth, through any carpets, floorboards or space that separate you from the earth.

Take as much time as you need to feel connected to the earth on a spiritual level.

Visualise the grounding energy from the earth like a white light, coming up through your entire body, cleansing and renewing – from the soles of your feet right to the top of your head – then outward, surrounding you in a beautiful, grounding light.

Once you feel grounded, cleansed, and renewed, slowly draw up your 'roots', and feel gratitude to Mother Earth.

Heart-Healing Bath Soak

This magickal bath soak is ideal when you just need to immerse yourself in magickal waters for a while and wash away the past, welcome the future, and heal your heart.

You will need: a quarter cup of Epsom salt, a quarter cup of coarse sea salt, rose petals, rosemary, a few drops of sandalwood oil

* Blend the ingredients together, stirring clockwise to attract healing, and set the intention that the salts will heal your heart and help you to move forward.

* Set the mood for your bath in whatever way suits you with your chosen music, candles etc. Add the salts to your bath, again stirring clockwise.

* Then, as you bathe in your magickal salt bath, embrace positive thoughts, imagine your life moving forward with joy, and feel the magickal salts washing away negativity, while welcoming joy and healing your heart.

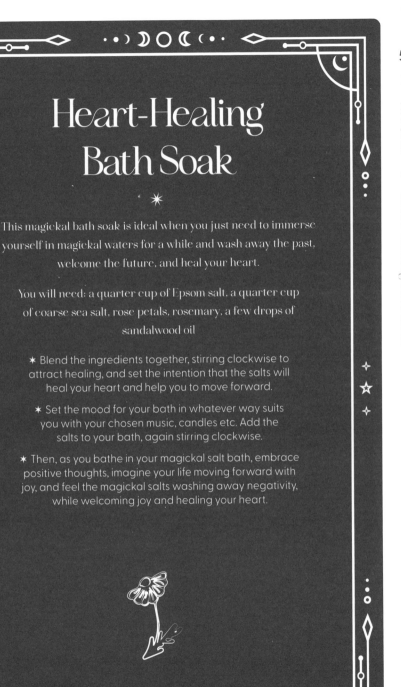

RITUAL

Hag

A wise old woman or elderly witch. Nowadays, the word hag has negative connotations – it has come to mean an ugly, or unpleasant old woman. However 'hag', much like 'crone', was once a positive title given to elderly women who were known for their wisdom or healing skills.

✦ ✶ ✦

Hag Stone

A stone with a natural hole running through it, believed to have magickal properties. Often found on beaches and near rivers and other natural bodies of water, a hag stone is formed when water seeps into a stone and gradually wears away at it until a hole is formed. If you find a hag stone, it is considered good fortune. Wear or carry the stone for luck or protection, or hang it in a doorway or window to keep negative energies at bay. Keep under your pillow to banish bad dreams. These are just a few ways to use this magickal stone. As the rock comes from the earth and is forged in water, it can also be used to represent the elements of earth and water on your altar.

✦ ✶ ✦

Handfasting

An ancient Celtic ritual in which the hands of a couple wishing to pledge their union, are tied together with fabric, cords, ribbon or lace, to symbolize the binding of their two lives and their commitment to each other. This is likely where the phrase 'tying the knot' originated. These days, in most countries, rather than being a legal marriage, it's a purely symbolic ceremony that is hugely popular among pagans and Wiccans.

Hearth Witch
aka Cottage Witch

A witch whose practice is centred around their home and garden, and whose entire home is their sacred space. Hearth witches incorporate magick into most of their household tasks, and they are often very fond of crafts such as candle making, knitting, sewing etc, making the most mundane task magickal by working intentionally. Often accomplished healers, hearth witches will usually use plants from their own home or garden to create herbal remedies or nourishing meals filled with healing energy. Hearth witches live their lives in a mindful and spiritual way, appreciating the simplicity and magick of their hearth and home.

Hedge Witch

Similar to a hearth witch, a hedge witch's practice centres around the home, but most hedge witches specialise in herbalism. Hedge witches focus on personal growth and spirituality, and as well as working with plants in a practical way, they also feel a deep spiritual connection to nature and all plant life. They are often solitary witches, or work in small groups, and practice in a simple way without the need for elaborate magickal tools. Usually they have an interest in faeries (fay, fae, fey), and believe there is more to the natural world than the eye can see.

Herbalism

The study and practice of using plants medicinally, and in the case of witches, magickally. Traditional herbalism uses the leaves, roots or flowers of plants to either promote good health or treat ailments. Most witches, to some degree, include herbalism in their practice. Further, witches believe in the magickal properties of plants, even when not consumed or applied to the body, so they will incorporate them into rituals and use them in spell jars, charm bags and spell powders etc.

Herbology

The study of the medicinal qualities of plants. Often the words 'herbalism' and 'herbology' are used interchangeably, but the difference between them is that herbalism is the practice of using herbs and plants for medicinal purposes, and herbology is the study of the same. So, while a herbologist will learn what ailments a specific plant is good for, a herbalist will also study how it effects the human body, and how to use or administer it.

Hereditary Witch

A witch who is descended from a bloodline of witches, and who practices using the traditions and knowledge handed down to them through the generations. A hereditary witch benefits from the tried, tested and trusted spells and rituals that they have inherited, sometimes in a family grimoire or Book of Shadows, or else simply by the witch being included in the family traditions from a young age, and learning through practice.

Hex

A magick spell or charm which is intended to bring harm.
To hex someone is to put them under a spell that will attract
misfortune, ill health or hardship. Witches who believe in the
Threefold Law will think carefully before hexing someone,
as they consider that it will ultimately come back to them.

High Priestess

Though this can vary depending on tradition and coven,
the leader of a coven is often referred to as the High
Priestess. The High Priestess embodies intuition, creativity
and the divine feminine. Having dedicated her life to
the craft, studied, trained and incorporated it into her
everyday life, she will have earned this title and status.
The High Priestess is a teacher, a leader and a healer.

Horned God (The)

The primary male Wiccan deity. While there are many
cultures who worship Gods who have horns or antlers – and
some pagan religions, and even some Wiccans, worship more
than one horned God – when we hear 'The Horned God' in
relation to a singular God, chances are that it's a reference
to the Wiccan deity. The Horned God is associated with the
wilderness and the life force that runs through all animals,
and is the most common depiction of the masculine Divine
in Wicca. Commonly worshipped as a male fertility God, the
Horned God is synonymous with masculinity.

Hydromancy

The practice of divination by using water. Water's reflections, shadows and ripples make it an ideal scrying tool. Water has been believed to be a source of wisdom for centuries. Just like the crystal ball, scrying with water is more likely to be successful if there is some light involved to create shadows and light, where images can present themselves. Hydromancy can be practised anywhere there is water, from the bathtub, to the lake, to a dedicated scrying bowl.

Here is an example of the scrying bowl method, since it is accessible to all:

Candles are the perfect light source in this instance, for their flickering will introduce shimmers on the surface of the water. Some like to use darkened water, so feel free to experiment. Darkened water can be created by soaking herbs in the water, then straining before use. Give the water a stir (clockwise) with either a quartz wand or your index finger, and then gaze into the ripples. Use your intuition to interpret any images, messages or symbols that present themselves. Sometimes you will 'sense' an image, more than you can 'see' it. Pay mind to this; divination is more than just visual and your intuition is all-important.

Setting Boundaries Candle Spell

✶

We must never feel selfish if we don't have the time or energy to keep on continually giving of ourselves. It's important to be able to set boundaries and stick to them! Here's a candle spell to help you to do just that.

You will need: a small grey candle, dried rue

✶ Place the grey candle in a suitable holder, and circle it with the rue, making sure that the rue is not in danger of catching alight, even when the candle burns low.

✶ As you light the candle, state the following:

"My boundaries will be clear,
I will set them without fear,
I will protect my energy
And choose only what's best for me."

✶ As the candle burns down, feel yourself being empowered to say 'no' when you'd like to, and know that moving forward, you can do this without any feelings of guilt.

RITUAL

Imbolc

aka Imbolg or Saint Brigid's Day

One of the eight sabbats, Imbolc is a traditional festival, celebrated midway between the Winter Solstice and the Spring Equinox. This is a time for purification, cleansing and planning.

Incantation

A spell or charm that is spoken, sung or chanted, which is intended to have an effect on a person or object or outcome. Incantations can be spoken words – in the witch's own language and charged with intent – or they can be a chanting of noises or made-up words that have meaning and power known only to the witch casting the spell.

Intention

The setting of a purpose or goal. Magick is nothing without intention. Every spell or ritual starts with the setting of this intent: thinking or stating what you desire, and what outcome you are hoping for and expecting from your magick. You can set your intention by visualising the desired outcome, through incantations or via meditation. Some witches sit with each item they'll be using in their craft, pour their energy into them, and infuse them with their purpose. Some witches journal about their intentions; they will write down exactly what they intend and expect, and some will even write this in the past tense as if it has already happened. Whatever way you choose to set it, intention is at the core of your magick.

Invoke

To call in a higher power for help. This is usually calling on a spirit, deity or the power of the elements for some kind of assistance, inspiration or protection. Unlike evoking (where we call to attend), when we invoke something, we are calling something *in*, meaning into our auric field, our body, our mind or a vessel.

Simple House Blessing or Cleansing

First, do a physical clean and declutter – remove anything from your home that you feel gives off negative energy, and surround yourself with things that have a positive feel to them.

You will need: incense and an incense burner, or aromatic herbs or resins

* Open all of the windows and doors to let the light and fresh air flood in!
* Don't forget to open all closets and drawers so you can be sure you have cleansed every space.
* There are several incenses, herbs or resins you can use for this cleansing, depending on your desired result. See *Smoke Cleansing* to help you select one.

✱ Set the incense, herb or resin to smoulder, following the manufacturer's instructions if using an incense burner, or in the case of natural herbs, see *Smoke Cleansing*; and carry the burner or herbs safely to ensure no smouldering ash can drop to the floor. As you burn your chosen incense, herb or resin, walk around your rooms – always starting at the top of your home, moving downwards and out towards the exit – working counter-clockwise as your intention is to banish negativity. Blow the smoke carefully into each corner and every cupboard. As you do so, state your intention (feel free to use your own words, or those below):

**"Negative energy leave this space,
love and light take its place."**

✱ Once your cleansing ritual is complete, close all windows and doors, and as you do so, again, state your intent:

**"Only good may cross through here,
my space remains light and clear."**

Your space is now cleansed!

Jinx

An unlucky or malevolent thing, person or force. If someone or something is 'jinxed' they or it attract misfortune. Unlike a hex, a jinx is more of an unintentional curse – it is thought that you jinx someone or something accidentally.

Kitchen Witch

Similar to a cottage or hearth witch, but with their craft more centred around the kitchen. It is common for a kitchen witch to have an altar of sorts right there in their kitchen, and their most important magickal tool is usually a wooden spoon or spatula which they use to stir their intention into their meal making and food preparation. Their cooking and baking are at the core of their craft and they do this with great care and intention, and using seasonal natural organic ingredients that they often produce themselves. They regard their cooking as alchemy, and use the magickal properties of the ingredients, along with their own energy, to create magick. Anyone can practice kitchen magick – making a simple cup of tea or coffee can be magick if done with intent.

Knot Magick

A magick spell cast by the tying of knots in a piece of string or cord. A witch will think of (or meditate on) what spell they'd like to cast, and visualise a positive outcome. As they do so, they firmly tie knots into a piece of string. Sometimes they will chant, or state aloud their intention as they tie each knot, and often they will tie in charms, ribbons, or other objects to represent their intent. They will then keep the knotted string in a suitable place, or in the case of attraction or protection knots, hang it in their home. So long as those knots stay firmly tied, the spell is alive. To break the spell, they can simply untie the knots.

Know Your Worth Confidence Spell

✳

If you have been feeling anxious, depressed, or have been suffering from low self-esteem, here's a spell that can remind you just how amazing you are! (Though we always advise seeking professional advice if you feel you need it.)

You will need: a small yellow candle, bergamot essential oil, a carrier oil such as olive or coconut oil, a mirror, paper and a pen

✳ Before you begin, mix a few drops of the essential oil with a carrier oil such as olive or coconut oil. Six drops in 10ml (⅓fl oz) of the carrier oil makes a safe 2% dilution - add just three drops if you have sensitive skin, and check in advance that you have no allergy to prevent you using bergamot. Never use undiluted essential oils on your skin.

✳ Sit in front of the mirror and see not just your outer reflection, but your inner soul-beauty too. Remember times in your life when you have felt accomplished and write down reminders of these – maybe you created something wonderful, or helped a friend through a bad experience... anything positive you can remember, write it down.

✳ As you write, relive how you felt in those times of accomplishment. Note down your positive personality traits – for example, I am driven, I am focused, I am kind – anything about you that you consider to be a positive attribute.

✳ Anoint the candle with bergamot essential oil and light it.

✳ As it burns meditate on all those wonderful things you've just written down. Start to feel truly positive and happy with yourself.

RITUAL

YOU ARE INCREDIBLE!

★ Once your meditation is over, anoint your wrists and forehead with the dilution of the uplifting bergamot oil and repeat the following:

*"I see my value, I know my worth,
I am confident and strong,
I shine my light upon this earth.
Anxiety be gone."*

Whenever you feel anxious or down, re-read those affirmations, anoint yourself with the oil, and feel your confidence returning.

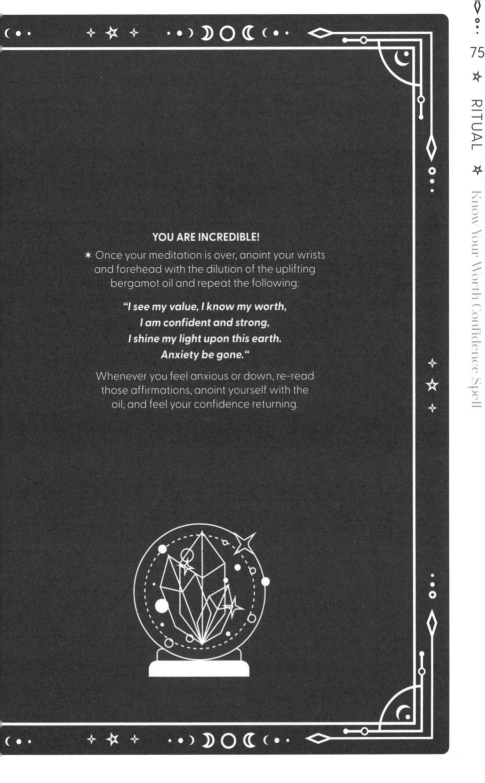

Litha
aka Summer Solstice or Midsummer

One of the eight sabbats, Litha celebrates the longest day and the shortest night of the year. This is a time of joy and celebration, as the sun is at the height of its power. Many witches use this time to form an intentional connection with nature by spending time outdoors, grounding, swimming and foraging etc.

Lithomancy

The practice of divination using the reflections and patterns formed by stones, crystals or charms, which are cast by the diviner. The simplest form of lithomancy is to use 'meaningless' stones and decide what they mean before they are cast. For example, you could assign 'no' to a red stone and 'yes' to a green stone, and ask a simple yes or no question. When cast, the stone which lands nearest to you gives you your answer. Similarly, you may assign a stone to yourself and give the other stones meanings, then the one that lands nearest your 'self' stone is the one to pay attention to. Another method is to cast your stones onto a cloth or grid designed for this purpose. Some experienced readers enter a trance-like state, cast their stones and watch for images, symbols or messages that may appear in the light and shade, and patterns of the stones. Often, using their intuition, they will 'sense' an image or message, more than they will 'see' it.

Lughnasadh
aka Lammas

One of the eight sabbats, celebrated midway between the Summer solstice and the Autumn equinox, Lughnasadh is the celebration of the first harvest; it is a time for giving thanks for any abundance that you have in your life.

Mabon

aka Autumn equinox

Celebrated at the time when night and day, dark and light, are equal. Mabon celebrates the period of rest after the labour of harvest, and is a time to reap what you've sown and celebrate the fruits of your labour.

———————————————————————— ✦ ✴ ✦

Magick

Magick with this spelling was first used in the 1600s and is an early English spelling for 'magic'. It has more recently been adopted to differentiate stage magic and illusion, from the very real magick associated with witchcraft.

———————————————————————— ✦ ✴ ✦

Magick Circle

A magick circle is an energy field that some witches choose to surround themselves with before their magickal workings begin, to create a sacred, protective space for them to work their magick. Some also like to cast a magick circle before meditating. The magick circle provides protection, since it is cast with the intent of only positive energies being allowed to enter. This means that when the witch opens themselves up to energies, they are protected from negative ones. Not only this, but the circle contains and amplifies their own personal energies making their magick more powerful; the circle is almost like a cauldron for brewing up powerful energies!

———————————————————————— ✦ ✴ ✦

Maiden

Many of the Wiccan traditions honour the Triple Goddess, where each aspect of the Goddess represents a different stage in a woman's life. The Maiden is the first stage of that life, a time of youthful enthusiasm. She is associated with the waxing phase of the moon, and is young, vibrant and open to learning and growing.

Manifesting

Attracting a thing or an outcome by the use of magick, positive intentions and belief.

There are many different manifestation spells and rituals, but the art of manifestation is as follows:

✷ Have a clear vision of what you desire.

✷ Send this request out into the universe.

✷ Act to work towards that goal, knowing these actions will be rewarded.

✷ Believe that what you desire is already yours, and that it is on its way.

Being successful in manifesting is truly a state of mind, because we really have to believe in the outcome – the minute self-doubt comes into play, we are anti-manifesting! Believing in our own powers is at the very heart of everything in witchcraft, and manifesting is no different.

Meditation

The practice of being mindful and 'in the moment', of focusing your mind on a particular thing, and clearing it of the clutter of scattered thinking. Meditation is a technique that is used to relax, reduce anxiety and stress, and promote a sense of wellbeing. It is useful in witchcraft as it helps you to focus your intention and visualise your desired outcome, without the interference of cluttered thoughts. There is more than one way to meditate – it isn't always sitting cross-legged and breathing deeply – here are a few examples:

Breathing Meditation: Keeping in mind that longer exhales are calming and longer inhales are energising, spend a while focusing on your breathing. To energise yourself, ensure that your inhales are longer than your exhales, and for relaxing and calming yourself, ensure that your exhales are longer than your inhales.

Dancing Meditation: Put on some music and dance! Dance free of your ego – let yourself be moved only by the rhythm of the music. Yell, shout, jump, whatever feels good! In doing this you can achieve a euphoric meditative state, where your mind is free and you have surrendered entirely to the music.

Gazing Meditation: Find a natural object to focus your gaze on – this could be a tree, or a flower or a flame. Fix your gaze on this object and clear your mind of all else, slowly achieving a meditative state of natural relaxation. When using a flame, be sure to allow yourself to blink as normal, and if your eyes are sensitive to light, choose an alternative thing to focus your gaze on.

Slow Pace Meditation: Often we are so rushed that we don't have time to recharge. Try slowing everything down to half speed: shower slowly, walk at a slower pace, eat slowly and thoughtfully. Slow down your everyday tasks, focusing only on what you are doing, and do it mindfully.

Standing Meditation: In today's modern world we rarely take the time to stand still. Stand with good, straight posture, with feet facing forward, shoulder-width apart, and mentally scan through your body from top to toe, releasing tension as you go. Focus only on your body. This need only take a few minutes, but it's a great way to ground yourself and start your day free from stress and tension.

Medium

Someone who can transmit information to and from the spirit realm via paranormal channels. Mediums are a gateway to the world beyond life, and they will pick up on messages being sent by spirits. The extrasensory powers of a medium grant them the capability of communicating with those who have passed, and other ethereal spirits. This isn't always voluntary; they can't always choose when a message will come through.

Merry Meet

A greeting often used by Wiccans, witches and pagans. Akin to "pleased to meet you", it means they are happy to see each other. Often, on parting, they will also say "merry meet again", which means "I'll be happy to see you again".

Mindfulness

Focusing your consciousness on being fully aware and present in the moment.

The practice of mindfulness can prevent us from becoming overwhelmed, or from over-thinking, or overreacting. It teaches us to be aware of our thoughts, feelings, body, mind, and all of our senses, in order to create a feeling of calmness. For example, eating our meal in front of the TV, while distracted by our favourite show, means we won't notice the textures, aromas, or even the taste of our meal to its fullest extent. Were we to sit and enjoy the meal just for itself, taking the time to experience it slowly and mindfully, noticing all of its qualities, the meal could be a calming, relaxing experience in an otherwise hectic day. It is in taking the opportunities that present themselves many times a day that we learn to be more mindful in all aspects of life, and this eases anxiety and stress, and encourages us to enjoy our life in that moment.

Money Bowl

A spell to attract wealth, which is cast by adding certain items to a bowl with a candle in the centre.

Here's how to set up this spell:

✶ Place a candle in the centre of a suitable bowl. Safely encircle it with dried herbs, plants or flowers believed to attract wealth, such as mint, cinnamon, bay leaves or chamomile. Add in crystals that align with your intention such as citrine, green aventurine or clear quartz. Use your creativity to add in anything else you feel can work, such as coins, small notes or affirmations. While you are creating your bowl, be sure to keep setting your intention.

✶ Light your candle and as it burns, visualise the abundance you seek and firmly set your goals and desires.

✶ You can 'feed' your bowl over the coming days, adding in more and more items imbued with your intention to make the spell more powerful.

You can keep the bowl until you feel it has served its purpose.

Moon Magick

Magick associated with the moon. Working with the different moon phases is an important part of many witches' practice. The full moon, for example, is a time for intense magick, a time of extra potency. During the full moon witches will take ritual baths, cleanse and charge their crystals, and perform their most important magick.

The new moon is all about new beginnings and a perfect time to cast spells for moving forward or starting new projects. The waxing moon is the phase where the moon grows and should be used for spells for growth or increasing self-esteem, and attraction spells such as love or wealth. The waning moon is the phase where the moon becomes smaller and should be used for banishing, letting go, and removing unwanted negative things and energies from your life.

Moon Phases

The changing views of the moon. There are eight moon phases as follows: new moon, waxing crescent, first quarter, waxing gibbous, full moon, waning gibbous, third quarter, and waning crescent. Witches who work with lunar energy will cast different spells, perform different rituals, or set different intentions, depending on which moon phase is present. Here are a few examples:

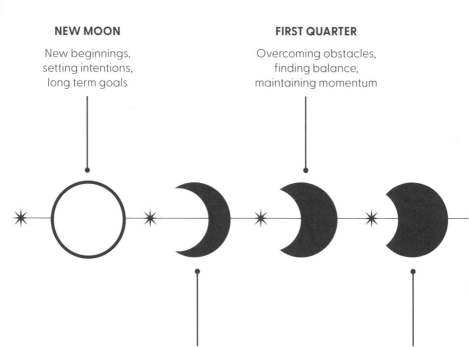

NEW MOON

New beginnings, setting intentions, long term goals

FIRST QUARTER

Overcoming obstacles, finding balance, maintaining momentum

WAXING CRESCENT

Manifestation, action, planning

WAXING GIBBOUS

Determination, patience, perseverance

MOON PHASES

FULL MOON
Fulfilment, gratitude, high energy

THIRD QUARTER
Boundary setting, transition, forgiveness

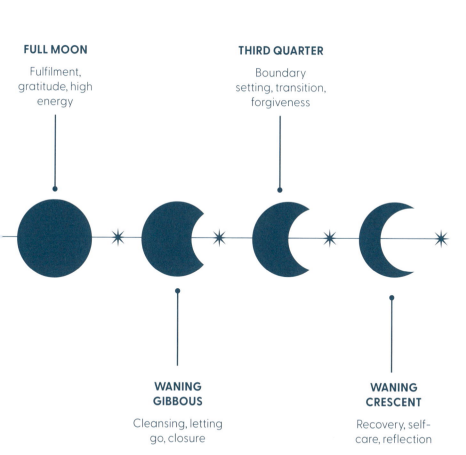

WANING GIBBOUS
Cleansing, letting go, closure

WANING CRESCENT
Recovery, self-care, reflection

Moon Water

Water which has been charged with the moon's lunar energy.

How to make moon water:

You will get your best results on a full moon – but it's not essential to wait for one!

✴ Fill a jar or similar container with water. If you plan to consume the water, it is safest to use bottled or filtered water and a container with a lid.

✴ Place the jar in the moonlight and surround it with crystals, charms or herbs that match your intention. You can also draw sigils on the jar to help focus your energy and intention. The colour of the jar can also help, for example a green jar would help with things like prosperity and a pink jar would help with self-love and relationships.

✴ Leave your jar overnight.

✴ Your moon water is ready to use.

Some uses for moon water:

✶ Add moon water to your tea or coffee (please use bottled or filtered water). This is a simple way to add more magick to your daily routine if you're tight on time.

✶ Water your plants with it.

✶ Add it to your bathwater for ritual baths.

✶ Wash your crystals and altar tools with it. Please research your crystals and make sure they can come into contact with water without damage. For example, selenite would dissolve, calcite can fade and hematite can rust.

✶ Wash your hands with the water before casting spells or performing rituals.

✶ Add the moon water to potions and elixirs.

✶ Place it on your altar to represent the element of water, or to amplify your intentions.

✶ Create essential oil perfume.

✶ Create an aura cleansing spray. Add it to a spray bottle and spray your aura every morning to cleanse your energy before starting your day.

✶ Use it in magickal floor washes.

✶ Use it for facial steams or add to your aromatherapy diffuser, add different essential oils to match your intentions, for example, add some rose or lavender to help with self-love.

✶ Cook with it. Infuse soups and other magickal recipes (please use bottled or filtered water).

Mother

Many Wiccan traditions honour the Triple Goddess, and each aspect of the Goddess represents a different stage in a woman's life. The mother is the middle stage of life, between the maiden and the crone. Represented by the full moon, she is the embodiment of feminine sexuality, fertility, motherhood and creation. A woman does not need to have children to embrace the role of the mother; there are many ways to embrace this nurturing and creative stage of life.

— ✦ ✷ ✦

Mystic

A person who seeks truth and knowledge from places beyond the scope of normal, intellectual thought. Similar in some ways to a medium or psychic, but not exactly the same. A mystic may not tell fortunes, or speak with the dead (though some do), but they engage in spiritual practices to gain insight, connect with the Divine, and obtain knowledge and a greater truth than that of the physical world. Mystics have no desire to simply 'believe' in something, they seek to connect with that which they believe, and become one with it.

— ✦ ✷ ✦

Mysticism

The belief in, and practice of, connecting to the Divine, and the ability to attain knowledge and insight, which may be unavailable to others, from this union. The practice of mysticism involves entering an alternate state of consciousness in order to achieve a oneness with the Divine, by acts such as meditation, chanting mantras or deep prayer.

Anti-Anxiety Salts

✴

Create these magickal bath or smelling salts to aid you in times of high anxiety.

You will need: a small bottle, equal parts Epsom salts and sea salt, a few drops each of ylang ylang oil (healing and calming), lavender oil (soothing and healing) and bergamot oil (confidence and courage)

✶ At a time when you are feeling at ease blend the salts and oils together, counter-clockwise, with the intent to banish anxiety, and giving thanks for their magickal, calming properties.

✶ Keep them sealed in their bottle until you feel you need their calming powers.

These can be used as a smelling salt, or added to your bath water.

Necromancy

A magickal practice that involves communicating with the dead. Necromancers may summon spirits during ritual magick in an effort to conjure apparitions or visible entities in order to communicate with them. Or else they may use divination tools such as Ouija boards, tarot cards or crystal balls to communicate with the dead. The practice of necromancy stems from the belief that the dead have valuable knowledge of the past, present and future. From this, necromancers hope to gain knowledge, insight or information into the future in order to influence the path of things to come. Many consider this to be a dangerous practice due to the potential for inviting negative spirits, or at least angering the spirits who may resent being called back into the living world.

Neo-pagan

A member of a contemporary religion who practices traditions other than those in the mainstream. Neo-pagans are not all witches, as this term encompasses many different religious groups. What all of these groups have in common is that they are reviving ancient practices and blending them with new traditions.

Nocturnal Witch

A witch who practices after dark. Believing they are more powerful at night because this is the time they feel more energised, a nocturnal witch embraces the darkness and does all their spell-work and rituals after dark. They will work with lunar energy, make moon water and take advantage of the power of the night.

Norse Witch

A witch whose craft centres around the Norse tradition, and who worships the Norse Gods and Goddesses. During divination, a Norse Witch will often work with runes carved with the Norse alphabet, and may also carve these runes into candles during candle magick. Some Norse witches believe in the Nine Worlds which, according to Norse Mythology, make up the universe, and they may incorporate these realms into their magickal workings.

Numerology

The belief and study of the divine or mystical connection between numbers and events; the faith in numerical patterns and their meanings. In numerology – based on the theories of the Greek mathematician Pythagoras – all things, including names and dates of birth etc, are reduced to numbers. It is believed by many who practice numerology that these numbers have a meaning and importance, and can help to guide us through life, and even be used to predict or give insight into the future. The use of numbers as a divination tools is known as arithmancy.

Negativity Banishing Potion

Create a magickal potion to keep negativity at bay, and protect you from bad energies.

You will need: one tablespoon each of raspberry leaf, dandelion root and Irish moss, safety pin, one cup of water and a pan, tea strainer or sieve, small glass potion bottle

* Heat some water in a pan and stir in the herbs and safety pin. Allow to simmer.

* As the potion simmers, chant the following:

> *"A potion to banish all that's wrong,*
> *Negativity and misfortune be gone.*
> *Attract to me, love and light.*
> *A potion to bring all that's right."*

* After simmering for ten minutes, turn off the heat and allow to cool completely.

* Strain the potion and pour it into a suitable potion bottle.

* You can now pin the safety pin discreetly inside your clothing to take extra protection everywhere you go.

The potion can be added to a ritual bath, used as a floor wash, an aura spray, or a room spray etc. Use within 24 hours.

RITUAL

Occult

Relating to hidden knowledge, the supernatural, the mystical and the magickal. When someone speaks of 'the occult' they are speaking broadly about any practice, belief or study that is outside of the field of mainstream practice. This can include witchcraft, divination, parapsychology and so on.

Omen

A sign of the unseen or things to come. Contrary to popular belief, an omen is not necessarily a bad thing, it is simply something that happens that is a sign of things to come. Many omens become superstitions, such as the belief that if it rains on your wedding day it's a sign of good fortune, or that a bird pooping on you means good luck is coming, or an itchy ear means you are being talked about. An omen is a happening that gives you a clue to unseen or future events.

Oneiromancy

The interpretation of dreams to gain insight into the past, present and future. Dreaming has long been considered a means of supernatural or divine communication, and since ancient times those who believe this have sought meaning. A gifted oneiromancer can see things in their dreams as they actually happened. The most powerful oneiromancers can see things in their dreams before they happen, and in doing so predict the future.

Onomancy

aka Nomancy

An ancient form of divination based on the querent's name. There are several methods of onamancy, for example: one method is based on numerology, another is based on the character strokes in the letters.

Oomancy

aka Ovomancy

Divination using eggs. There are many methods of egg-reading. One method is to take an egg white and drop it into warm water, the resulting shapes formed by the egg can be read in much the same way as tea leaves are read. Some practitioners use cold water and let the egg white sit for a while before interpreting the shapes formed.

+ ✳ +

Oracle

A message from the Divine, or a person through whom the Divine speaks. An oracle delivers messages, imparts wisdom, and gives advice based on their communication with the Divine. Oracles often have insight into the future, and they may be sought out to give counsel based on their prophesies.

+ ✳ +

Ostara

aka Eostre or Spring Equinox

One of the eight sabbats, typically celebrated on the equinox, or the full moon thereafter. Ostara celebrates balance, rebirth and new beginnings. This is a great time for purification spells, and spells for fresh starts, or new projects etc.

+ ✳ +

Ouija Board

aka Spirit Board

A board through which people attempt to speak to spirits. Originating in the late 1800s a Ouija board is usually made of wood and has each letter of the alphabet on it, along with the numbers 0-9, and the words 'yes' and 'no'. Sometimes 'hello' and 'goodbye' are also included. Those using the board place their fingers on a small, heart-shaped piece of wood or plastic, known as the planchette. During a séance they ask questions and the planchette moves about the board to spell out the answers given by the spirits that come through.

Wish Come True Candle Spell

✶

Here's a simple yet powerful candle spell to help you to manifest your desires!

You will need: a small white candle, cloves, star anise, lodestone oil, something sharp

✶ Take your sharp object and etch into your candle anything which represents your wish: sigils or words, whatever feels right to you.

✶ Anoint your candle with lodestone oil, brushing the oil on the candle towards yourself while stating the outcome you wish to attract.

✶ Place your candle in a suitable holder and circle it with star anise and cloves, arranging them to avoid any risk of them catching alight, even when the candle burns low.

✶ Light your candle.

✶ As it burns, visualise your wish being realised, feel the emotions and gratitude as you know your wish will soon come true!

RITUAL

Pagan

A person who holds religious beliefs outside mainstream religion. Pagans believe that nature is sacred. They connect spiritually with the earth, observing the changing of the seasons and the natural cycles of birth, growth and death. Some pagans worship multiple Gods and Goddesses, others worship only Mother Earth. Pagans do not necessarily all share the same beliefs and values as each other; they follow their own spiritual path without feeling the need to conform.

Palmistry

aka Palm Reading

Fortune telling through the study of the palm of the hand. Palmists read the shape of a person's palm, the undulations (or mounts) and lines, and other physical attributes. There are five main lines to be read, a multitude of smaller lines and seven mounts. It is believed that the information gleaned from analysing these can be used to tell the querent's fortune, and give insight into the past, present and future.

Path

A spiritual journey. The word 'path' in relation to witchcraft is the journey you take in order to become spiritually fulfilled and enlightened. There is no 'one true path' in witchcraft, and no set rules for the path you must follow. Each of us is free to decide the path we wish to take.

Pendle

A town in Lancashire, England, famous for its witch trials of 1612. Twelve people from Pendle Hill and the neighbouring region were accused of witchcraft, and eleven cases went to trial. All but one of the accused were found guilty and hanged. Such accusations were rife and there were many such trials between 1450 and 1750, during which time tens of thousands of people were executed. The Pendle witch trials are famous because the number of accused who were hanged together was unusual in England.

Pendulum

A divination tool used for dowsing. A dowsing pendulum is usually a rock or crystal hanging from a chain or cord, though they can also be made of wood or metal. This can be a very simple method of divination, especially when seeking simple yes or no answers.

Here is the simplest way to use your pendulum:

Hold the pendulum by the chain or cord and allow the tip to settle on the palm of your other hand. Remove your palm slowly ensuring the pendulum remains steady. If you do not have a pendulum board or cloth, you can simply ask a yes/no question that you already know the answer to, and see which way the pendulum swings. That allows you to ascertain the direction of your pendulum's swing for 'yes' or 'no' responses. Then you can ask questions where the answers are unknown, and see what insight the pendulum offers.

If you require more information you can buy or create a pendulum board or cloth, which will not only have 'yes', 'no' and 'rephrase' marked on it, but can also show the letters of the alphabet, so more in-depth answers can be spelled out depending on the letter the pendulum swings to when a question is asked.

Pendulums are often used to locate missing or lost items. To do this ask the pendulum to guide the way to the lost item, and follow the direction of its swing. For something lost further afield, you can hang the pendulum over a map and watch it hone in on a specific area to focus your search.

The main thing to remember when using a pendulum is to do so with an open mind, and try not to involve your 'will'. Your own will is very powerful and can muddy your readings if you are 'willing' the pendulum to swing or move in a certain way.

Pentacle

The pentacle, a five-pointed star depicted within a circle, has long been used by witches as a symbol of protection. The five points of the pentacle representing the five elements of earth, air, fire, water and spirit – the five things essential to sustain life. The circle surrounding them contains and protects, and also connects the five points indicating that earth, air, fire, water and spirit, are all connected. The pentacle has had some negative press over the years due to its inclusion in horror films, where it has been associated with devil worship, but in reality, the pentacle is a peaceful and protective symbol.

Pentagram

A five-pointed star without the circle. In witchcraft, like the pentacle, it is often used to symbolise the elements, but the pentagram has a wider range of cultural and symbolic associations.

Poppet

A doll made to represent someone in order that you can cast spells on them, or aid them, through magick. Traditionally, these were often carved from natural materials such as roots, or branches, but in modern witchcraft they are more likely to be mindfully sewn from cloth and stuffed with herbs that relate to the intention of the witch creating them.

Potion

A liquid with magickal or healing properties. This can be a bath potion, an anointing potion, or even a simple herbal tea that has been brewed with magickal intent.

Precognition

Seeing, or being aware of, future events. Those with this gift have knowledge of future events without predicting them by using reason. Sometimes information on upcoming events comes via dreams, others receive this knowledge by entering a trance-like state, and some have premonitions while being awake. This information can come through to some people as clearly as if they were watching a movie. However in many instances, the gifted receive only fleeting glimpses or images that are more difficult to make sense of; and others have surreal dreams featuring images or symbolism, which can be hard to decipher. Frustratingly, for some, these glimpses of the future can only be linked to the event in hindsight, after the moment has passed.

Psychic

Someone with the ability to connect with others on a soul level in order to obtain insight into what the person is thinking or feeling, or to pick up information about the person's past, present and future.

Psychography
aka Automatic Writing

Psychography is the art of writing without conscious thought. It is a tool used by psychics and clairvoyants to transcribe the messages they receive. It can take some practice to allow yourself to access the state of mind required to do this, since you have to have a very clear mind, free of all distractions. It is necessary to switch off all rational thought completely, enter a trance-like state, and connect spiritually with your higher self and the incoming messages.

All you need for this is a pen or pencil and some paper – then connect with your tools, and disconnect from everything else.

Note down the question you'd like to ask, then relax your body and mind. This is not something you can rush, so take your time. If you are able to make a connection, messages will flow through your subconscious and onto the page.

Psychometry

Psychic vision through touch. Psychometry works on the principle that objects hold on to energy, and contain a psychic impression of people who have touched or held them. Those with the gift can speak of the history of an object, and those who have held it, simply by touching it.

Pyromancy
aka Fire Scrying

There are many variants on basic pyromancy. Most involve throwing something into the flames, such as salt (alomancy), plants (botanomancy) etc, but basic pyromancy uses only fire. Bonfires are an excellent method since they are lit outdoors, where there's a natural breeze, and have an abundance of flickering flames to gaze at and decipher. Coal or log fires are also an excellent scrying tool. However, a candle or candles can work too, though it's advisable to crack open a window, so there is a breeze – a flickering flame, rather than a very still flame, is desirable.

✴ Always exercise good sense when working with fire. Check that flammable materials (and children and pets) are kept safely away from the flames, that there is adequate ventilation if the fire is indoors, and don't take any risks with adding accelerants. Never leave a flame unattended.

✴ Gaze into the fire as you ask your questions, then notice the appearance of the flame, and any sparks or shadows, or hisses, crackles or other noise. You can use your intuition to decipher what you see and hear, keeping in mind the following:

✴ If your fire proves difficult to ignite for no apparent reason, then this could be telling you that a particular venture or relationship is going to take more effort than imagined.

✴ The intensity of the flame – how fast it is consuming the wood, coal or wax – can tell of the speed of a particular outcome.

✴ Flames which burn more ferociously in the centre advise focusing on your current situation or problems before moving on. There is something central in your life that requires your immediate attention.

✴ A spitting or spluttering flame can suggest either negative gossip, or something unsaid that will build resentment if not voiced.

✴ It is a good omen if the flames are light and clear.

✴ As you gaze into and around the flame, look for images, shapes and symbols to appear. Children are particularly good at recognising images in fire and shadows, so invite your child-like intuition to play, and take note of what you see. And ultimately, as the fire burns out, it may offer you a final message in the smoke that it leaves behind.

Quarters

The quarters represent earth, air, fire and water, and correspond to the four directions of North, East, South and West respectively. The elements are called upon by some traditions to bring balance and elemental energy to their magick circle, and this is called 'Calling the Quarters'. Depending on the tradition involved, what is specifically being invited can vary: for some it is spirits or entities associated with each element, for others it is the energetic qualities each element holds.

Querent

The person inquiring, or asking questions during divination. While in the world of law, the word 'querent' means 'complainant' or 'plaintiff', in the world of divination it refers to the person asking questions of the practitioner.

Retrograde

When a planet appears, from here on Earth, to have reversed its direction. This is actually an optical illusion, but in astrology a retrograde can spell trouble!

Mercury, being the planet which rules communication and expression, goes into retrograde three to four times every year, and these retrogrades are blamed for everything from miscommunication and arguments, to technological issues.

Ritual

A ritual, like a spell, is a set of actions to bring about a desired result, but it is more involved than a spell and tends to bring religious or spiritual beliefs into the magick. This can be done in many ways, such as calling on deities, chanting or dancing etc. Any spell can be developed into a ritual by incorporating your own personal spiritual practices.

Rune

A letter from any one of the runic alphabets. Runes date from around 100AD, and the best known and most often used runic alphabets are the Elder Futhark, the Anglo-Saxon Futhorc, and the Younger Futhark. Runes are used in witchcraft in the form of stones for divination, or as magickal sigils to add power to spells; for example, carved into candles for candle magick, or written down to be added into spell jars and charm bags.

Rune Stones

These are traditionally made of stone, but can also be made from crystal or wood. While there are a few different runic alphabets, the most common is the Elder Futhark. Used for divination, traditional sets of rune stones have 24 pieces with symbols on them, and one blank. If you draw a blank stone, this can tell you that you already have the answer and that you should seek it within.

As with most divination tools, runes do require that you use your intuition to decipher the messages they carry, as the meaning of each rune can sometimes feel 'vague' in relation to the question posed; for example, one stone can symbolise 'fertility' but also 'wealth', 'energy' and 'good fortune'. It is likely that one of these meanings will resonate more than the others, so let your intuition guide you.

Here's how to perform a simple single stone reading:

* Clear your mind.

* Focus on the question you would like to have answered.

* Hold the bag of rune stones in your hand.

* Ask your question and take a stone from the bag.

* Read the symbol written on the stone. That answers your question.

If you need further clarification, take another stone from the bag. If you find you still need clarification, place the stones back in the bag, reshuffle them, and rephrase your question.

Runes can also be 'cast':

Traditionally it is said that the runes should be cast onto cloth, and that you should select the runes you are going to read while you are looking up to the universe.

Another method is to throw the runes onto a piece of cloth and to only read the ones that have fallen face up.

Past Relationships Cleansing Spell

✴

Sometimes it can be difficult to move forward because some of the vestiges from your past relationships remain stagnant in your home. Here is a quick cleansing spell to remove the energy of relationships past.

You will need: bayberry oil (for healing), dried rose petals (for heart-healing), white candle (for cleansing), candle holder

★ Grind your rose petals into smaller pieces, suitable for candle dressing.

★ Anoint the white candle with bayberry oil (smoothing the oil away from you, as you are banishing residual energy).

★ Roll the candle in the ground rose petals.

★ Stand the candle in a suitable holder to carry it safely, and light it.

★ Carrying the candle, slowly move through each room in your home and state the following with intent:

**"With this light, this room I clear
of energy that lingers here.
What once was, is now behind.
I reclaim my home, heart and mind."**

You can now move forward knowing that the energy of past relationships will no longer linger in your home, heart and mind.

RITUAL

Sabbat

A sabbat is one of the eight celebrations or festivals recognised and celebrated by Wiccans and many (but not all) pagans and witches. Beliefs can vary regarding the precise timing of each celebration, depending on the celebrants own religious or spiritual beliefs, and based on distinctions such as lunar phase and geographic hemisphere. The sabbats are as follows:

* Yule
* Imbolc
* Ostara
* Beltane
* Litha
* Lughnasadh (Lammas)
* Mabon
* Samhain

Sacred

Devoted to a specific deity, religion or practice. For example, a witch's altar could be considered their sacred space, and the tools used in a witch's practice – if they are important and dedicated for use only during magickal workings – could also be considered sacred. The path a witch takes, is their sacred path.

Salem

A city in Massachusetts, USA, famous for its witch trials. Salem is synonymous with witchcraft following the hearings and prosecutions of alleged witches in 1692, which saw over 200 people being accused of practicing witchcraft. This resulted in thirty people being found guilty, and of those, nineteen (fourteen women and five men) were executed by hanging. One man, Giles Corey, died as he was relentlessly tortured for refusing to enter a plea. While these trials and executions were not unique, such was the hysteria surrounding witchcraft in that region at the time, that it was the deadliest of the witch hunts in colonial North America.

Samhain

aka Hallowe'en

One of the eight sabbats, Samhain celebrates the thinning of the veil between our world and the spirit world. This is a time to celebrate and honour our ancestors and passed loved ones, and to communicate with them, leave offerings for them and remember them.

Scrying

Scrying is an ancient form of divination, which involves gazing into a surface such as a crystal ball, a mirror, water or flickering flames. There are no limits as to how and where, and with what tools, a person may scry. They may stare into the darkness, or up at the clouds, or drop ink into water, looking for any signs and symbols they can translate. Some people even talk of 'eyelid scrying', where they simply close their eyes and speak of what they see there. The images seen by the diviner can be fleeting, hazy or vague, but the intuition of the diviner helps them to discern and understand the scattered, fragmented images, and translate them into something tangible.

Practitioners gaze at their chosen scrying tool and focus on nothing else. This helps them to clear their minds, and enter a trance-like state. It is in this state that those gifted with vision can see signs, symbols and imagery, which can give them an insight into the knowledge they seek.

Sea Witch

With a strong connection to the ocean, sea witches draw from the power of the sea during their magick. Because of the duality of the ocean, they can draw calmness from it and also primordial, powerful energy! They may draw sigils in the sand and forage on the beach for shells, driftwood, seaweed, sea glass or hagstones. They may collect sea water that they then use in their craft. They may also work with spirits of the sea, and worship sea Gods and Goddesses. Like the ocean, a sea witch will be connected to, and work with, the cycles of the moon.

Séance

A gathering of people attempting to contact the dead. Sometimes a séance will include the use of a medium who will be a conduit for messages between our world and the other side. Without a medium, some will use a tool such as a Ouija board, tarot cards, a flickering candle or a pendulum, in order to communicate. Many consider this to be a dangerous practice due to the potential for stirring up unwanted energies and spirits.

Secular Witch

A witch who does not incorporate any religion into their craft. For a secular witch, witchcraft is a practice rather than a religion. They focus on the natural world, and the energy which surrounds and runs through all things. They will practice their magick without calling on, or worshipping deities.

Seer

A person with a deep spiritual insight, wisdom and knowledge, and the ability to see that which is hidden. A seer views the world from a spiritual standpoint and can see the meaning in things that may seem irrelevant or invisible to others. Some seers see the future through dreams, divination or visions.

Shadow Work

A practice which encourages you to process issues or parts of yourself that you may have been repressing, so that you may start to heal and to love the parts of yourself that you've been suppressing and rejecting. Some of us repress anger, trauma, grief, jealousy or stress, but those things then remain, waiting to be triggered when we least expect it. There is no question that holding these things inside of us may serve us well 'in the moment', but can be extremely damaging to us if we fail to work through them. Ignoring our shadow-self can cause low self-esteem, self-loathing, self-sabotage, and it can impact our relationships with others. Facing our fears, by working through our trauma and negative emotions, can allow us to begin to heal and to understand ourselves on a deeper level. There are many methods of shadow work, from meditation, to journaling (often using prompts to ensure you work on those parts of yourself that need attention), to artistic expression. Shadow work is an extremely emotional and difficult practice, and should be done gently. However, if this causes great distress you may prefer to seek professional therapy.

+ ✷ +

Sigil

A sigil is a symbol used to represent a desired outcome. Commonly created by using lettering, and condensing that lettering down to a single symbol. Sigils are charged, during their creation with the intent of the practitioner or witch. They can then be used in magick: etched into candles, written in salt or herbs, sewn into poppets or charm bags – the uses of sigils are only limited by our imagination.

+ ✷ +

Skyclad

To be naked, particularly during ritual magick. Some believe that clothing interferes with our ability to connect with nature, and therefore that magick is more powerful when performed naked, when we are fully able to connect with the elements.

Smoke Cleansing

Smoke cleansing involves burning herbs, wood, incense or resins in order to rid your space of negative or stagnant energies. There are several incenses, herbs or resins you can use depending on your desired results – here are some examples:

Lavender: calming and protecting, attracts peace and love

Dragon's blood: Banishing and protecting

Peppermint: Purifies, calms and heals

Sandalwood: Protects and heals, will attract serenity and peace

Frankincense: Protects and attracts good fortune

Cedar: Protects, purifies and heals

To cleanse using smoke from your own herbs, you can place the herbs on a lit charcoal disc in a suitable fire-proof container and allow them to smoulder and smoke.

Alternatively, you can make your own herb bundle in the following way:

Take lengths of herbs and bundle them together. Secure the bottom with string or twine, and wind this up the length of the bundle, and back down in a criss-cross pattern, tying it off at the base. Hang the bundle in a suitable space for a few weeks until the herbs are completely dried. To use your bundle, keeping it over a suitable container to catch any smouldering ashes, you can light the end, then after a few seconds blow out the flame. You can now use the smoking herb-bundle for cleansing.

Smudging

A cleansing ritual involving the burning of sacred herbs (often white sage). The herb is burned to cleanse and purify the body, mind and soul. Smudging is a closed practice of many Native American and other indigenous cultures, i.e. only to be practised by those cultures.

So Mote It Be

A common way of ending a spell or ritual. Meaning 'so must it be', or 'so shall it be'. Often used at the end of a spell or ritual, for example in candle magick as the candle burns out; while making a charm bag as the bag is tied shut; or as the final words in a spoken spell.

Solitary Witch

A witch who practices alone. A solitary witch may practice one or many of the different traditions but rather than be a part of a coven, or practice with other witches of a similar path, a solitary witch works alone.

Solstice

One of the two times of the year when the sun is farthest north or south of the equator.

For witches, the longest day of the year is known as the Summer solstice, or Litha, and the shortest day of the year is the Winter solstice, or Yule.

Soothsayer

One who speaks the truth. A fortune teller, or someone with great intuition; this may be anything from a tarot reader, to a prophet, to someone with a precognitive gift.

Sour Jar

Often used as a form of revenge or retribution, a sour jar is a vessel created to literally sour someone's life. It is a jar in which you place something to represent your target plus a base of vinegar, and to this you can add other items to annoy and irritate such as chilli or thorns. Witches who believe in the Threefold Law will think carefully before creating a sour jar, as they consider that the ill-will will ultimately come back to them.

Spectre (Specter)

A ghost, spirit or other apparition.

Spectral Evidence

In the 16th and 17th century, during the witch trials, people alleged that spectres (specters) of the accused would visit and torment them, and they submitted this 'spectral evidence', as if it were irrefutable. Of course, if believed, it was impossible to disprove. Though this evidence alone was not considered sufficient for conviction, it carried some weight and was taken very seriously by some judges, no doubt resulting in the execution of innocents.

Spell

A set of actions to bring about a desired result. Whereas a ritual generally incorporates spirituality or religion, a spell is simply the setting of intentions while carrying out actions. A spell can be a very simple form of magick, examples of which are practiced every day such as the act of blowing out birthday candles and making a wish, or writing your desire on a bay leaf and burning it to send your wish into the universe. Spells are not always simple – they can be complicated, just like a ritual – the difference is the absence of religious or spiritual ceremony.

Spell Bottle

aka Spell Jar

A vessel filled with things that represent your intention, with the purpose of achieving a pre-determined outcome. A bottle or jar is filled with herbs, crystals, affirmations, amulets etc, which have been charged with your intention. This is then kept in your home or on your altar, or located depending on its intended use. From time to time you can sit with your bottle to reaffirm your intention and to recharge it. Once it no longer serves, any herbs can be offered back to the earth with thanks, and the bottle, crystals and amulets etc can be cleansed for re-use.

Spellcraft

The creating and casting of spells.

Spell Powder

A powder containing magickal properties. Spell powders are created by taking dry ingredients, such as herbs, seeds or dirt, and grinding them together to create a powder that can then be used for spell work. Always use blends that are appropriate for the spell you intend to cast – dried rose petals work great in a love powder, for example.

As you grind and blend the powder, fill this with your magickal intent and belief. The more you intend and believe in the outcome, the more you infuse that into your powder, and the more powerful the powder will be.

USING YOUR POWDER

There are many ways to use powders in your spell work. Here are just a few of them:

Blowing: Place the powder on the palm of your hand and blow it into the air. If casting a spell for someone (for example a healing spell) even if that person is far away, you should blow in the direction that they are.

Drawing: You can draw with your powder to mark out the circle for rituals, to make magickal patterns or sigils on the altar, or to mark out visually the intentions of a spell.

Dressing: You can dress many items with spell powder: items such as ritual candles, love letters, business cards, money, application forms etc.

Wearing: You can wear your powder like a talc (assuming you are not allergic or sensitive to the ingredients used) or add it to charm bags etc. Wearing the powder is a very good way of taking the magick with you to important meetings, events or rituals.

Summerland

A realm where some pagans believe they go after death. Usually depicted as a natural place of woodland, babbling brooks and enchanting gardens; a place where the sun is always shining. The Summerland is considered a tranquil place for peace and rest. Some believe this is a place to rest before reincarnation, for others it is a place of eternal peace.

Letting Go Fire Ritual

Occasionally we need to rid ourselves of something that no longer serves us, so that we can move on in peace. Here's a fire ritual to help you to do just that.

You will need: a pinch of chamomile, a pinch of lemon balm, paper and pencil, fireproof bowl, matches or lighter

- ✷ Take your piece of paper and note down anything you wish to let go of.
- ✷ Blend your chamomile and lemon balm counter-clockwise while imagining your life free of the unwanted object, entity or issue.
- ✷ Fold the herbs inside the paper, and place it in the fireproof bowl.
- ✷ Set the bowl down in a safe place, and carefully set your paper/herb bundle on fire. As it burns, state the following:

"I release what I no longer need,
Rid myself of it at speed.
Fire and smoke set me free,
As I will it, so mote it be."

- ✷ Do not leave the fire unattended. Once it has burned out, allow the ashes and the bowl to cool completely, then take the ashes far away from home and bury them – walk away without looking back.

Talisman

An object which is believed to bring good fortune, protect its bearer, or have other magickal powers.

Tarot Cards

Decks of card have been used as a divination tool for centuries, and today tarot is one of the most popular divination methods.

The standard deck is a 78-card deck consisting of 22 major arcana (numbered 0-21) and four suits comprising of 14 cards for each suit.

While there are countless different takes on the tarot deck, the traditional suits are as follows:

Cups: These tell of emotions, creativity and intuition. They appear in readings to tell us about our feelings, relationships and emotional connections.

Pentacles: These tell of career, finances and material possessions. They appear in readings to give insight or advice into practical matters.

Swords: These tell of actions, words and intellect. They appear to encourage us to assert ourselves, make decisions and act.

Wands: These tell of motivation, energy, charisma and passion. They appear in readings to tell us about new ideas, finding purpose, and focusing our passion and spirituality into moving forward.

In order to effectively read tarot, it is wise to learn the basics of the meanings of the cards, and then allow your intuition to take over.

When reading intuitively, it can often be that a part of an image jumps into focus. This feature may have little or no relation to the accepted meaning of the card, but it may mean something to you. If you are open to reading intuitively, the meanings for the cards seem limitless, and once you start to follow your instincts, you will learn to trust your intuition and will see what needs to be seen.

Tasseography

aka Tasseomancy

Divination that involves reading patterns in tea leaves. Some practitioners will read the patterns in coffee grounds or wine sediments, but most commonly tea leaves are used. In the case of tea leaves, a cup of tea is made without using an infuser or strainer, the querent then drinks the tea. From this point the method can vary, but usually the tiny amount of liquid that remains in the cup is swirled and poured away so that the patterns that remain in the tea leaves can be read. Although most readers prefer to use a plain white cup, in the late 19th century special cups were created to make the reading of leaves easier, and those cups are still produced and used to this day.

Theban Script

aka Theban Alphabet or The Witches' Alphabet

This is a writing system which has been utilised by some witches to disguise their words so they cannot be read and understood by anyone unfamiliar with the script. The script can be used in the same way as sigils, or it can be used to write an entire Book of Shadows (though this would only be recommended if you are fluent in the script as reading your own text could become problematic).

Thelema Witch

Witches who practice the Thelema tradition. Thelema was founded in the 1900s by well-known occultist, Aleister Crowley. The religion is based on finding your own individual purpose and discovering your true calling or destiny, referred to as your 'True Will'. The key principle of having the freedom to do as you desire is stated as "Do what thou wilt shall be the whole of the law". Magick is at the core of Thelema, along with other practices such as yoga and meditation.

Third Eye

The third eye is the sixth of the seven chakras. Usually depicted on the forehead – between the eyebrows but slightly higher – the third eye is believed to give you a sight or perception beyond your ordinary vision. With the third eye open, your intuition is heightened, your 'hunches' will be correct. You will know things instinctively, like who is calling you, or which path to take, or whether a person you meet is a good person. As the third eye opens, instances like this become commonplace and you will be more decisive, and more confident to go with your gut feeling. Working with your third eye can open the door between the self and the spirit, and make you feel more connected to the universe.

Threefold Law
aka The Rule of Three

An ethical guideline which promotes the theory that whatever you put out into the universe, either positive or negative, will come back to you multiplied by three. In Wicca and some other pagan religions, this is for many a strictly held belief. Some believe that three times is not literal, but alludes to the fact that your energy will return to you as many times as is necessary for you to learn from it. In either case, for those who believe, this encourages them to practice magick only for good, and never practice magick with malice or to cause harm.

Threshold

The bottom of a doorway or entranceway. You have to cross a threshold to enter any room. In witchcraft this is important as many witches practice 'threshold magick'. This means they cast spells that are intended to affect or protect the home, or anyone who crosses the threshold.

Tincture

A medicinal liquid containing concentrated plant extracts and ethanol or alcohol. There should be at least 20% alcohol present in order to preserve the tincture, but anywhere between 20% and 60% is common. Tinctures are very potent and are administered either in drops, or having been diluted.

Here is one way to prepare a tincture:

Start by adding your chosen herbs to a jar, then cover them entirely in your alcohol, ensuring there is enough liquid to cover the herbs and more besides. Add a lid and seal tightly. Place the jar somewhere warm and let it sit. The jar should be kept like this for a month and shaken regularly. After a month, open the jar and strain the liquid into another bottle or jar through a piece of muslin. The herbs can be discarded and the tincture kept in a cool dark place until needed. At all times, the tincture should be clearly labelled and kept out of reach of children.

Tinctures are usually administered as a drop or two under the tongue, and should not be applied to the skin or eyes. IMPORTANT: Using any tincture can carry risks, as even medicinal herbs can have side-effects in some people, especially if they interact with other medication. As with everything in this book, although I give the definition, it is the individual's responsibility to look into any and all side-effects of the tinctures they prepare.

Traditional Witch

A witch who practices traditional witchcraft that preceded the modern traditions. A traditional witch will have studied the history of witchcraft and will work with time-trusted spells and ancient knowledge. Though they may incorporate some modern ideas and work with modern tools, the root of their magick is in practicing the ancient traditions.

Tree of Life

The tree of life symbol has many different interpretations depending on different traditions, cultures and religions. Most often depicted as a huge tree with an abundance of strong roots, its branches and roots forming a circle, the tree of life generally symbolises the circle of life and the connection between all things. It's a symbol of strength, growth and rebirth. It is such an important symbol in such a vast number of cultures and religions that there is a seemingly endless amount of mythology and lore surrounding it.

Triple Moon
aka The Triple Goddess

Representing the three aspects of the Goddess: the maiden, mother and crone, and honouring each stage of the female life cycle, the Triple Moon symbolises the three, united.

Triquetra
aka The Trinity Knot

An ancient symbol of three arches which interconnect to form a knot. Though its true origin remains a mystery, it is believed to be over 5000 years old, and throughout time has been used in architecture, ironwork, and engravings. The symbol is recognised by many traditions, cultures and religions, and is sometimes used by neo-pagans and Wiccans to symbolise the Triple Goddess, or as a symbol of protection.

Calming Bath Ritual

This ritual uses the element of water to soothe and calm.

You will need: chamomile, passionflower, water and pan, bathtub

★ Boil some water and stir in the chamomile and passionflower. Stir clockwise as you say the following:

*"Soothing water and healing flowers,
Soothe my soul with your magickal powers."*

★ Allow the flowers to infuse for five minutes and then strain, keeping the floral-infused water.

★ Fill a bathtub and add the floral infusion, stirring clockwise and once again stating:

*"Soothing water and healing flowers,
Soothe my soul with your magickal powers."*

★ Soak in the tub, and feel the magickal waters soothing your soul and washing away any anxiety or stress.

RITUAL

Village Witch

A witch who gives help and guidance to their local community. A village witch will offer their magickal services for the greater good of the village, by creating charms, casting spells and making herbal remedies etc. Such a witch may follow any tradition in addition to being a village witch, they may be Wiccan or a kitchen witch, for example. The term 'village witch' simply means they work their magick for the good of the community.

Vibration

The energy emanating and oscillating from all objects. The atoms and molecules that make up all matter vibrate, and different objects vibrate at different frequencies. When brought together the vibration of one object can affect the vibration of another; this is the basic premise behind things such as crystal healing. The vibration of a living being is often referred to as their 'aura'.

Visualisation

A very important part of witchcraft, visualisation is the conjuring of mental images that will assist you in your goal and add power to your magick. If you can visualise a desired outcome, it is easier to set your goal and direct your energy and focus towards manifesting it. Whether you visualise just the ultimate outcome, or you visualise each step on the path to that outcome, the more detailed your visualisation, the more it will serve your magick.

Wand

Traditionally made of wood – but can also be made of metal or rock, and often set with gemstones and crystals – a wand is a rod used to channel and direct energy, and cast protective circles. Unlike an athame, a wand has a gentler energy, which is used to invite and encourage rather than to command.

Warlock

A man with magickal powers. A male practitioner of witchcraft, magick or sorcery. Some male witches prefer to identify as a witch, others identify as warlocks or wizards.

Wheel of the Year

A symbol depicting the annual cycle, marking the eight pagan festivals or sabbats, as shown here. The solstices and equinoxes may also be included.

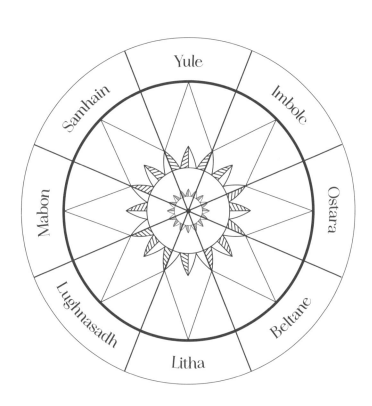

NORTHERN HEMISPHERE:

Yule (Dec 20-23),
Imbolc (Feb 1),
Ostara (Mar 20-23),
Beltane (May 1),
Litha (Jun 20-23),
Lughnasadh (Aug 1),
Mabon (Sep 20-23),
Samhain (Oct 31).

SOUTHERN HEMISPHERE:

Yule (Jun 20-23),
Imbolc (Aug 1),
Ostara (Sep 20-25),
Beltane (Oct 31),
Litha (Dec 20-25),
Lughnasadh (Feb 1),
Mabon (Mar 20-25),
Samhain (May 1).

White Magick

Magick with good intent, or to counteract evil. Practitioners of white magick use their magick for selfless purposes.

Wicca

A modern religious movement, derived from many pre-Christian religions and incorporating many pagan beliefs, which was introduced in the 1950s by Gerald Gardner. Though Gardner himself referred to it as 'witchcraft' or 'the craft of the wise', at some point in the 1960s Wicca became the accepted name for the religion. At the beginning, people would join the religion by invitation into a coven, having gone through an initiation. In the 70s, after books were published to teach people how to initiate themselves into the religion, the movement grew in popularity. Some Wiccans worship deities from many mythologies and cultures, but most primarily worship the Triple Goddess, the Horned God and the Earth. A nature-based religion, Wicca celebrates eight seasonal festivals called 'sabbats', and its followers are encouraged to honour the changes of the seasons.

Wiccan

A practitioner or follower of Wicca.

Wiccan Rede

A poem which states the morals of Wicca, and has also been adopted by other similar witchcraft-based faiths. The most commonly used part of the Rede, often referred to as 'the short Rede' is the closing line: "An ye harm none, do what ye will". The long Rede has evolved and organically changed a little over time, so there are now several versions with slight variations, and seemingly no single definitive one.

Widdershins

Anti-clockwise/counter-clockwise. Used in magick to banish. For example, if making a healing broth you would stir it counter-clockwise to banish illness. If you were making a charm bag for 'letting go', you would blend the herbs counter-clockwise etc.

Witch

A person who practices witchcraft. There is so much diversity among witches, their beliefs, their religions and the way they practice, that defining a 'witch' in any other way than 'a person who practices witchcraft' would be unthinkable. Each witch follows their own magickal path, and it is not for me to define who they are, or what they do.

Witch Ball

aka Spirit Ball

A witch ball is a hollow sphere, traditionally made of green or blue glass, which is hung in the home to ward off evil spirits, negative energy, hexes and ill-fortune. Originating in England in the 17th century witch balls are still used by witches and superstitious folk today. They hang in windows and doorframes to protect against negative influences and bad luck.

Witch Hunt

A hunt for, and purge of, people who have been accused of witchcraft. Witch hunts were prevalent in Europe, and to a lesser extent America, between 1450 and 1750, and during this time tens of thousands of people were executed. Overall it is estimated that over 75% of those killed were women, and more than 40 of those executed were children. Often those accused were healers, herbalists, or simply women who were well known for being quarrelsome and aggressive.

+ ✳ +

Witchery

The practice of witchcraft.

+ ✳ +

Witches' Bells

A protective charm made from bells. The ringing of bells has long been used to clear away stagnant and unwanted energy from the home. Witches bells are a cluster of bells, designed to hang on your door as a protective charm and ring whenever anyone enters, ensuring whoever is paying you a visit doesn't bring negative energy with them.

+ ✳ +

Witching Hour

A time of night when witches are at their most powerful and spirits are most active. This is considered to be the time when the veil between worlds is at its thinnest. There are different beliefs as to when exactly the witching hour is; some say midnight, and others believe it is around 3am.

+ ✳ +

Wizard

A man with magickal powers. A male witch. Some male practitioners prefer to identify as a witch, others identify as warlocks or wizards.

Yule

aka Winter Solstice

> One of the eight sabbats, Yule is the time when the darkness gives way to the sun, and days start to get progressively longer. Yule is a celebration of rebirth, renewal and the continuation of life. A perfect time for candle magick, rest and self-care.

Zodiac

> A region of the sky that is divided into twelve zodiac signs: Aries, Taurus, Gemini, Cancer, Leo, Virgo, Libra, Scorpio, Sagittarius, Capricorn, Aquarius, and Pisces.
>
> Your own zodiac sign depends on where the zodiac is in relation to the sun on the day that you are born. Astrologists believe that an individual's zodiac sign can be used to tell of the person's personality, and that deeper study can give insight into their past, present and future.

About the Author

Deb is a practicing witch from Yorkshire, England. Specialising in divination and spellcraft, her spells and rituals are performed by witches worldwide.

Co-founder of Witch Casket, the magickal monthly subscription box, which she founded with her daughter Ella, she is fulfilling her dream of making witchcraft more accessible.

Through her work, Deb has helped witches across the globe to find their spiritual path, be more empowered, and to live their lives authentically.

Always creative, Deb has written for many years, first as a screenwriter, and more recently in the creation of the self-published books, distributed exclusively through Witch Casket.

Deb is delighted that her passion for writing and her love of the craft, have resulted in fulfilling another lifelong dream of becoming a published author with this book, *The Witch-ionary*.

Through magick, hard work and self-belief, Deb has overcome trauma and hardship, and is manifesting the life she always imagined. Her mission now is to write a series of books to guide others to do the same.

143 ✭ ABOUT THE AUTHOR

A DAVID AND CHARLES BOOK
© David and Charles, Ltd 2024

David and Charles is an imprint of David and Charles, Ltd
Suite A, Tourism House, Pynes Hill, Exeter, EX2 5WS

Text © Deb Robinson 2024
Layout © David and Charles, Ltd 2024

First published in the UK and USA in 2024

Deb Robinson has asserted her right to be identified as author of this work in accordance with the Copyright, Designs and Patents Act, 1988.

All rights reserved. No part of this publication may be reproduced in any form or by any means, electronic or mechanical, by photocopying, recording or otherwise, without prior permission in writing from the publisher.

A catalogue record for this book is available from the British Library.

ISBN-13: 9781446313909 hardback
ISBN-13: 9781446313916 EPUB

This book has been printed on paper from approved suppliers and made from pulp from sustainable sources.

Printed in China through Asia Pacific Offset for:
David and Charles, Ltd
Suite A, Tourism House, Pynes Hill, Exeter, EX2 5WS

10 9 8 7 6 5 4 3 2 1

Publishing Director: Ame Verso
Commissioning Editor: Lizzie Kaye
Managing Editor: Jeni Chown
Editor: Jessica Cropper
Project Editor: Jane Trollope
Head of Design: Anna Wade
Designer: Marieclare Mayne and Jess Pearson
Pre-press Designer: Susan Reansbury
Illustrations: Adobe.Stock.com
Production Manager: Beverley Richardson

David and Charles publishes high-quality books on a wide range of subjects. For more information visit www.davidandcharles.com.

Follow us on Instagram by searching for **@dandcbooks_wellbeing**.

Layout of the digital edition of this book may vary depending on reader hardware and display settings.